The
Black Walnut Farm

A Book of Short Stories

Ted A. Woodworth

Author of *The Black Walnut Farm Series*

Illustrated by
Edie Woodworth Hewgley and
Tabetha Hewgley Brett

Emerald Ink Publishing
Hot Springs, AR

The Black Walnut Farm

Editor, Ellen Bennett

ISBN-13 # 978-1-885373-52-6

Library of Congress Cataloging in Publication Data:

Woodworth, Ted A.
Black Walnut Farm : a book of short stories / Ted A. Woodworth ;
    illustrated by Edie Woodworth Hewgley and Tabetha Hewgley
    Brett
    p. cm.
ISBN 978-1-885373-52-6 (trade pbk. : alk. paper)
1. Woodworth family. 2. Woodworth, Ted A.--Family. 3. Farm
    life--Indiana. 4. Indiana--Biography. I. Title.
CT274.W65W66 2005
977.2'042'0922--dc22

                                                        2005003797

Emerald Ink Publishing
        Printed in the United States of America

Teachers of writing are missing a good bet if they fail to share the writings of Ted Woodworth with their students. He writes the correct way—the way he speaks. He doesn't use two voices. He uses a homey style, obviously enjoys putting words together, and writes about things he experiences or knows of. The result is prose that takes the relaxed shape and rhythm of conversation.

Bob Moore,
Educator, lecturer and journalist
Louisville, Kentucky

As an experienced educator who grew up in a country village in Maryland, I have read this book with great pleasure and informed delight. It contains the real stuff of life and should appeal to the millions of older persons who grew up in rural America as well as their grandchildren. I see the same basic motivation as is found in the Laura Ingalls Wilder stories: to capture a way of life before it dies in the memories of those who lived it.

Richard E. Martin,
English and social studies teacher
LaGrange, Indiana

The Black Walnut Farm will be read and enjoyed by many people. You have a wonderful talent and I admire you for using it. I marvel at your ability to arrange your memories in story form. Keep on using the talents God has given you.

Ted Woodworth's former school teacher,
Amos O. Hostetler
Topeka, Indiana

The Black Walnut Farm is very touching, funny, loving and folksy—little stories of a family in the country in the late 1920s and early 1930s. It was a matter of family survival in those days and I remember them well. Ted brings out what was the American farm in the Great Depression. He's doing what every granddad should do for his grandchildren. He catches a little of his family background and saves it for them. It's little pieces of American history.

Donald R. Beaty
Former Educator, County Government Official
Arcadia, Michigan

ACKNOWLEDGEMENTS

For some time now, my daughter Edie has urged me to write down the stories I told her and her sister Becky, when they were children. Later, I told them to my son, Terry. Edie wanted her children and grandchildren to hear them, too.

I want to thank her for editing the book, and her and her daughter Tabetha for the illustrations.

Thanks, too, to my wife, Zena, who contributed stories of her own and for her advice on each and every story I wrote.

Nor am I forgetting the memory jogs given me by my brothers, Lloyd and Charles, as well as my sisters, Edie and Mary.

Many others contributed, like Kenneth Forgue and Nobby Johnson, and I want to express my appreciation to them.

Thanks, also, to my Amish friends for helping me re-live some of my memories.

Ted A. Woodworth

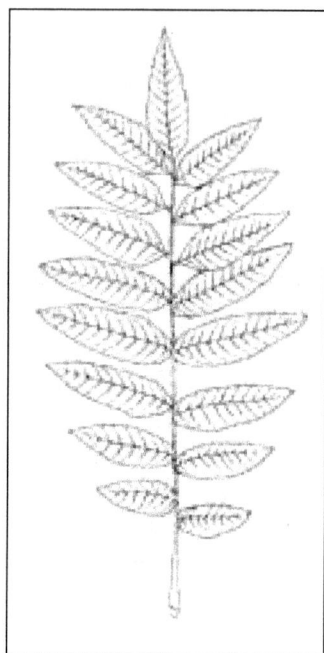

Contents

I'm Leaving You, Cecil!

*A*ll of my stories are based on fact, or at least the way I remember how things happened. I try to get close. In this case, however, I'm not in a position to remember, because I wasn't even born yet. But, it's a true story — or the way it was told to me by others who were there.

My sister, Edie, was in charge of taking sister Mary and brothers, Charles and Wayne, to the neighbors, Hattie and "Rube" Foltz. Lloyd was sent scurrying across the fields to Grandpa Woodworth's house to let Grandpa and Grandma know that Mom's "time" had come. "Blessed event," some call it. Before it was all over, Mom didn't think it was much of a "blessed" event.

Grandma's job was to call Dr. Grubb and tell him to get out to the farm as quickly as possible. Mom would have preferred to have had Dr. Schrock, who had delivered her first five children, but he had died some time after Wayne was born.

Lloyd had to go to "The Black Walnut Farm," where my grandparents lived, because they had the nearest telephone. Not only that, but Dad wanted his mother to come over and help out. He was worried. Mom had gotten awfully big and he was sure she was expecting twins. "Only problem with that is there are no twins on either side of the family," Dad said.

"In that case, I'm going to have a monster," Mom said. She had had a lot of trouble and pain during the whole nine months.

Mom had only been to town to see Dr. Grubb a couple of times during her pregnancy. There wasn't a whole lot that doctors could tell expectant mothers in those days. Virtually all expectant mothers gained a lot of weight. Then it took forever and a day to get rid of it, if they ever did. Mom was no exception. During a span of twelve years she'd had six children and so was always what we used to call "pleasingly plump."

My mother was a beautiful lady. Not just in her face. She had an inner beauty that some took longer to recognize than others, like her good sense of humor and that's important. In the meantime, back at the Foltz farm, my brothers and sisters were bragging to the six Foltz children that soon Mom and Dad would catch up with their folks. Each family would have six children. That was not unusual. Big families meant more hands to do the farm work. The young ones were now assigned by Mrs. Foltz to watch down the road for Dr. Grubb. Actually, the first car that came by was Grandpa's big Studebaker. He had bought it a couple of years before from Earl Fisher's Studebaker dealership in LaGrange. Grandpa pulled up in front of Foltz's to drop Lloyd off and then he drove Grandma on down the road about half a mile to help Mom.

Nobody remembers why it took Dr. Grubb so long to drive the six miles from LaGrange, but when he did finally make it, he was too late. In fact, Grandma got there too late. I got there too early. So. . . Dad delivered me. Neither the doctor nor Grandma was there yet when I entered the world, kicking and screaming. Mom said she wished I'd have gotten there a lot earlier because I was born half grown. Each succeeding child had weighed more than the last one and they tell me I weighed twelve and a half pounds. That's why she said, "I'm leaving you, Cecil . . . If you ever get me in the family way again. . . I'm leaving you!" And that's the story —except when Dr. Grubb returned to town he neglected to register my birth. The problem that caused me in later years is a story in itself.

History has a way of repeating itself. My granddaughter, Tabetha, and her husband, Stanley, decided to have their second child at home with the aid of a midwife. They had the good sense to attend Lamaze classes to learn all about the birthing of a child. Good thing they did, too. You guessed it. Little Michael Shey Brett arrived on the scene ahead of the midwife.

2

Dad's New Car — Cremated!

Since the events of this story took place the year before my birth, I have to admit the details came from the memory banks of my older brothers and sisters. They were there. Dad had three good years of high yielding corn and wheat crops during 1919 to 1921. Not only were the grain yields high, but the sows had outdone themselves with high producing litters. Along with that, the economy was right and prices were above average. Probably the biggest business transaction my Dad ever became involved in was the sale of his fat hogs, one of those years. With something between $400 and $500 of the proceeds, he bought a brand new Model T Ford. Brand new. Black in color, of course.

Since there weren't too many cars back in those days, there weren't many garages in which to keep them. Seems logical. Anyway, Dad kept his car in the barn. It was a reasonably good-sized barn with mangers for cattle and stalls for horses, some open space that could serve as protection for cattle, sheep and hogs, and doors to enclose the whole thing for complete protection in winter time. There was a cover over a single door that led into the side of the barn on the south side. This door faced the house. All along the east side where the smaller doors were, the ones where the livestock came in and out, there was an overhang across the whole lower long side of the barn. It made an excellent windbreak as well as a protection to keep snow from blowing into the barn when any of the doors were open.

It was as though the barn had been built into the side of a small hill. You could drive directly into either side even though one end was a story higher. The upper story had a granary on one side. Hay could be kept on top of it and on the other side it was just a hay mow. Between these two hay mows was room to keep farm implements—and the Model T Ford.

The events of the story about which I am writing occurred in the summer of 1921. My brother Lloyd was seven at the time. It happened after the threshing had been completed. The granary was bulging with a bumper harvest of wheat. A huge strawstack was in the barnyard. The hay mows were full to capacity. The farming tools were inside. So was the Model T Ford.

With summer school vacation nearly over, Dad had decided to take advantage of what help a seven-year-old could furnish. For that reason, Dad and Lloyd were way back in the woods with Barney, who wasn't much more than a colt, and Belle, his mother. They made quite a team. Dad had them hitched to a wagon and he and Lloyd were loading it with wood for the winter. That was a never-ending job. The house was not insulated as well as it might have been and the cookstove, as well as the heating stove, had a voracious appetite.

Then they heard it! Three shots rang out! Mom and Dad had arranged a signal. In an extreme case of emergency, Mom was to fire three pistol shots. This was it!

Dad ran as hard as he could to the edge of the woods. Then he could see it. The barn was on fire!75

Dad started running again as hard as he could toward the barn. Just as quickly, he reversed himself and headed back to Lloyd and the horses. By the time he got there, both Barney and Belle were picking up on the situation. They were aware that Dad was extremely excited. On top of that, they were north of the barn and the wind was blowing briskly from the south. They could smell the smoke.

Before they got to the edge of the woods, Barney had started to "run away." Dad finally got him stopped at the edge of the woods. Right then he tied both horses to a tree. Securely! He told Lloyd to stay with the horses and calm them. Then, he started running toward the barn—and the house—again!

The fire had started on the south side of the barn. Being where he was, Dad couldn't really tell if it was the barn or the house that was on fire, because he couldn't see the house. It was hidden by the barn.

Two horses were runnin' toward him in the lane leading to the barn. They were running from another smaller horse whose mane was scorched. The smell was driving all three of them crazy. That's when Dad knew for sure it was the barn that was burning. He passed the horses and kept on running.

Mom and the girls had started taking whatever they could carry out of the house. They were stacking furniture and clothing along the road out front. There was a chance the house would burn, too. But, not much—because the wind was blowing strongly from the south.

That's what had started the fire. The wind blowing from the south.

As usual, Mom had a fire in the cookstove. Chaff from threshing had collected on the overhang on both the south and east sides of the barn. Sparks from the chimney had blown onto the barn, starting the fire. The roof was wood shingle and it was dry. Whooooosh! Away it went!

Neighbors, from miles around, came a-runnin'. . . to see if they could help. They moved a lot of the furniture out of the house until it became obvious the house wasn't going to burn, because of the direction of the wind.

Sister Mary had carried out a jumper Mom was making for her. New! Mary said she mostly had to wear hand-me-downs from older sister Edie, so she sure didn't want to lose the only new item of clothing she had.

A couple of teen-age neighbors who carried out Mom's Crown reed organ tried to lift just one end of it later and couldn't. Adrenalin does wonders for people under stress.

From the Black Walnut Farm, Uncle Bela had cut across the back fields, riding his big black horse, to see if he could help. After some time, while counting "noses," he asked Dad where Lloyd was. "Good Lord!" Dad said. "He's still with Barney and Belle back in the woods. I'd forgotten all about him." It had been four hours since Dad had left him there.

Uncle Bela rode back to the woods where Lloyd was patiently watching over the horses and worrying about everybody at the house. After assuring Lloyd nobody had been hurt, they headed for the house with Barney and Belle.

The barn was nothing but a smoldering ruin.

Dad's new car had been cremated.

3

Our Dog "Shep"

*W*hen I was a little kid, they called me either Teddy or Teddy Bear. I had blue eyes and blonde hair, like my mom and dad. Wait a minute. I didn't mean my mom and dad had blonde hair. Mom's hair was black and Dad's hair was gray since I could remember. What I meant to say was that they both had blue eyes. I had the blonde curly hair.

I dressed like and I guess you could say I looked like any other little farm boy. But, I guarantee that there was a definite difference. Somehow, I could get into more trouble, by accident, than most boys could on purpose.

For instance: Let me tell you about something that happened the summer of the year that I turned four years old. It caused my mother to be very unhappy with me, but on the other hand, my dad thought it was so funny that he nearly laughed himself into a stroke of apoplexy.

During the 1920's, we lived on a 160-acre farm in Clay Township, LaGrange County, Indiana, that belonged to my grandfather, Fayette Woodworth. By we, I mean my mom and dad and my five brothers and sisters. I was the youngest.

Most of the farmers kept a few sheep and my father was no exception. Grandpa kept sheep on his farm, too. One thing that was different about my dad, though, was that he had his own sheep shearing machine and he could use it. He not only used it on his own sheep, but he took care of the neighbors' sheep, too. He was really good at it, but that's another story.

The only pets we had on the farm were cats (and every farm had cats) and a shepherd dog that we called Shep. Not very original, but that was it.

Shep was different than any dog that I had ever seen or have seen since. He used to smile. He did. He actually did. When he was happy to see somebody his tail would wag vigorously and he would bare his teeth in the finest smile you could ever imagine. Also, he kind of walked sideways, like he was embarrassed as he walked toward you. Sidled would describe it better. We loved him and wouldn't have traded him for any other dog in the whole world, not even Rin Tin Tin.

The summer that I turned four was an extremely hot dry one. Heat waves seemed to be everywhere. Even in the country, the air was almost stifling. No place, as they say, for man or beast. I can still see Old Shep lying in the shade of an enormous old black walnut tree that stood alongside the driveway to our house, his tongue hanging out as he panted like only a dog can pant.

Now, I can't say if it was Dad's idea or my brothers talked him into it or a combination of both, but Dad got out the sheep shearing rig and gave Shep a hair cut. It was something to see. They didn't shear his head and they left a three or four inch tuft of hair on the end of his tail. It made him look just like a little lion, but it sure did make him look cool.

Along about this same time, our neighbors, Ed and Barbara Miller, decided to conduct an experiment that was designed to save them money. She gave Ed a haircut. All the tools she had to work with were a pair of scissors and a comb. So, she had him sitting on a kitchen chair on the back porch with a towel draped across his shoulders.

Well, she started snipping away. She did pretty good on the sides, and from the front he looked just fine, but, in the back, well, Barbara just couldn't get it to come out even.

Ed was getting impatient because it was taking so long because he had work to do. Ed and his son Vanus owned and operated the only threshing machine in the neighborhood, so it figures that he had lots of work to do. Another reason he had agreed to let her cut his hair was that he didn't have time to get into town.

When she had the back finished she showed it to Ed—with the aid of mirrors front and back. Right away he could see that one side was cut higher than the other. "You don't have it even. Cut it higher on the other side," he told her. So she did. You guessed it. She took off too much and got that side too high. "Cut the other side higher" and so it went. The more he hollered at her, the more nervous she got and the more she botched up the haircut.

Finally, she stopped. In tears. She had cut all the hair off the back of his head. You could have drawn a line from one ear up over his head to the other and there would have been no hair behind it.

A few days after this, while I was playing with Shep in the front yard, I saw the Millers' big black Dodge touring car coming down the road toward our house, in a cloud of dust. I was pretty sure they were coming to our house because ours and the Reuben Foltz farm were the only ones on this stretch of road.

I rushed excitedly into the house to tell Mom. It was an event because we didn't get much company.

Mom went into what I've always thought was some sort of a magic act. When unexpected company appeared, Mom could clean the whole house, put on a clean apron, and make herself look crisp and fresh before they could get to the front door.

On this day, Mom could have saved her time because as Barbara drove up the driveway—she always drove—Shep and I hardly waited for the big Dodge to come to a stop before we jumped on the running boards. Shep, with his new haircut, on the driver's side, smiling up at Barbara and wagging his tail a mile a minute, and me on the passenger's side.

"Ed! Ed!" I called. "Take your hat off."

"What for, Teddy? Why do you want me to take my hat off?"

"I want to see your new haircut. Dad says you look just like Shep."

"Well, I never . . . !" muttered Barbara as she put the big touring car in reverse and backed out of the driveway.

As they drove away, in an even bigger cloud of dust than they had arrived in, I just knew I'd "done it again" and was "in for it."

Mom finally came out onto the front porch to ask what had happened to Barbara and Ed. Dad was standing behind the screen door.I was playing with Shep and acting innocent.

"Well, Teddy, was it Barbara and Ed or wasn't it?" Mom called to me. I decided I'd better "fess up," and so I told her what had happened.

When she grabbed me to drag me into the house to give me a sound threshing, she nearly yanked my arm out of the socket. And Dad? He ran out the back door laughing so hard he nearly died. Parents are sure hard to understand. Sheesh!

The moral to this story, of course, is, be very careful what you say in front of your children.

4

Boys Make Mud Pies, Too

*A*t times my grandchildren look at me kind of funny when I tell them a story about some experience I had when I was their age. It's not as though they doubt me, it's just hard for them to picture me as a little boy.

Even more difficult is picturing their grandmother as a little girl—and being punished by her mom.

Over the years, Zena has talked with some regularity about her Uncle Kiel and Aunt Elsie Crist. Then there were her cousins, Thelma and Milo. The two families must have been close friends as well as being relatives.

Zena's mother, Esther, and Aunt Elsie were sisters. That's how the families were related.

More than once, I heard that Uncle Kiel Crist was a "big man" in Kansas. He was a county commissioner, I think. And, had all kinds of connections with people up the ladder of Kansas politics.

Finally, I met them.

Aunt Elsie was a petite lady a little over five feet tall. Uncle Kiel stood three inches taller than me and I'm slightly over six feet. Also, he weighed a good solid 300 pounds. I had to agree with Zena. He was a "big man" wherever he happened to be.

The story our grandchildren found so hard to imagine took place when Zena was only about three. She said the family lived on the "Old Bumgardner Place," at the time. Aunt Elsie had stopped by with little Thelma, who was also about three. Dressed in her finest: white dress, white bloomers. The works.

Aunt Elsie wanted Zena and her mother to go along with her to pay a visit on another relative who was "ailin'." So—in short order Esther had Zena dressed in her white dress and matching' accessories, her "Sunday best."

Something delayed the mothers, giving the girls enough time to take off for their play area in the back yard. They promptly decided to make a "batch" of mud pies.

Zena had this pretend room with pretend furniture. The table was an orange crate. The chairs were blocks of stove wood. The pie pans were Mason fruit jar lids. An old abandoned galvanized pan served as a mixing bowl.

After stirring up dirt and water, they ladled it into the can lids with an old spoon that had somehow found its way out of the kitchen. A quick trip to the corn crib gave them another ingredient they felt was necessary for an appetizing touch. The kernels of corn were poked into the mud pies around the outer edge, kind of sideways. Sort of made it look like the way their moms always pinched the crust around the edges of the pies they baked.

Along about this time, their Mothers were ready to leave and came looking for the two girls.

Both were covered with mud!

Aunt Elsie caught Thelma and gave her a rare thrashing. Rare—because Thelma seldom did anything that required such punishment.

Zena ran for the windmill where she tried to wash the mud off her white dress, in the horse tank.

She wasn't very successful. Now, her dress was dirty all over.

So, she got a whalin', too.

The grandkids found that hilarious. Grandma getting a spanking!

But, back to making mud pies.

I tried to tell them, "Boys make mud pies, too."

In unison, Steve and Ted said, "nuh-uhh" or something like that. It means, "no, they don't."

What they meant was, they had never made mud pies.

Truth is, with a swing set, as well as bikes and toys and games, not to mention television, to keep them occupied, they didn't need to make mud pies. And they had each other. My brother nearest me in age was Wayne. He was three years older than me, and as far as I know, never made a mud pie in his life. Charles and

Wayne spent a lot of time together. Their age difference was about the same as that of Steve and Ted.

There's no two ways about it, I took my pie baking seriously. The pump and well couldn't have been more than twenty feet from the house, so getting water was no problem. The garden was about the same distance on the other side of the house. No problem getting plenty of good rich dirt to make mud.

Mother had given me a one quart aluminum pan, with a handle. It didn't set level on the stove, so she had given it to me. This made a good container to mix the dirt and water in.

But, that wasn't quite enough. Like any good cook, I tried to improve.

Now, I never thought of puttin' the pies in can lids. Instead, I just patted them out flat in my hand and laid them on a board to dry. They looked more like mud cookies. But I called them pies.

Dad was watching me one day and said, "Why don't you put some eggs in your batter? Then, when they dry, put frosting on them and call them cakes?" He was poking fun at me because he thought I was being a sissy.

But instead of discouraging me, he gave me an idea.

There was a lot of sand in the gravel on the road in front of our house. I managed to fill the quart pan with sand and brought it back to my "kitchen." There were some small stones in it, so I asked Mom if I could borrow her sieve.

"No!" was her firm answer. However, when I told her what I wanted it for, she found me a piece of window screen. It worked fine. In no time I had a nice pile of almost white sifted "flour." Some of this I mixed with my "batter."

Eggs! Yes, Eggs! Good idea. But, then, Mom would skin me alive if I took a chicken egg.

I know! Sparrow eggs! We had lots of sparrows in the barn. All I had to do was get up on top of the cow stanchions to reach their nests. Success! There were plenty of eggs. All I wanted.

Dad had said we had way too many sparrows and pigeons in our barn. I reasoned that if I took some of the eggs it would help lessen the bird population.

I remember the first time I put the eggs in my pocket as I gathered them. Not a good idea. My mother didn't like it much, either.

After she cleaned the smashed eggs out of my pocket, Mom gave me an old tin cup to gather the bird eggs in. It worked fine. Smart mom. The older I got, the smarter she got.

So then, I broke at least six speckled sparrow eggs into the batter to make one pie, or cake—if you'd rather. Mixing some of the sand in caused the batter to be a lighter color, too.

After the sun had dried the hamburger-looking mud pies real good, I'd sprinkle some sand on them. Made them almost white.

Uncle Marion would have said, "By Golly Ned! They look just like sugar cookies." And they did.

Recently, I told this story to my brother-in-law, Virgil Hayes. He said, "I never made any mud pies, but I did rob bird nests for a while. Got cured of it, though."

"How was that?" I asked.

"Stuck my hand in a nest one time, and pulled out a big bull snake."

That would have cured me, too.

5

Got Enny Gum?

*Y*ou just haven't lived if you've never seen pictures of the "flappers" of the 1920's. I've lived. I've seen them. I was there.

The two most beautiful flappers I knew were my sisters, Edie and Mary. They were both somewhat embarrassed at the length of the dresses, because they only came to their knees.

Both would blush coquettishly and tilt their heads slightly forward and to the left if they knew somebody was looking at them. And, especially if it was a young man.

You'd have to see one of those dresses in order to fully appreciate them. Most of the dresses were sleeveless and virtually without exception they had two inches of beaded fringe hanging from the hem. Usually, there was a fringe of these beads around the bodice, also. You should have seen my sisters when they danced the "Charleston." The beads would jiggle and bounce up and down or sway back and forth, depending on the movements of the dancer. In fact, they seemed to be gently moving all the time, even when the girls were standing still.

The dresses were brightly colored and the girls didn't have much need of makeup when they had them on. Their flushed faces and happy giggling were all they needed.

And necklaces! Great long strands of beads reaching to the waist or longer. The girls spent a lot of time toying with these beads or twirling them.

My sisters sure did enjoy their teen years. It seemed like every Sunday a couple of young fellows would "just happen to stop by." Most of the time they just visited or wound up playing ball with my older brothers. Often as not, they didn't work up enough courage to ask the girls even to go for a ride. Not always, but most times. It didn't take long before I knew one of their beaux were my favorites and I'd hope for their return.

One that came by to see my sister Edie was as rich as a Rockefeller, or at least I thought he was. I also decided he wasn't very smart. He wrote her a letter asking if he could take her to a show on Sunday night. She showed at least part of the letter to mom and dad. They exploded with laughter when they saw how he had spelled "show." He had spelled it "shoe." Between guffaws, dad said, "Maybe he wants to take you to see the little old lady who lives in a shoe."

The reason I was so convinced he was rich was that he normally drove a different car each time he came. And a new one at that. Expensive, too. Made dad's Model "T" look bad by comparison. One time he'd be driving an Auburn and the next a Cord. Like as not, the next time it would be a Duesenberg. One time he asked me to go for a ride with him and Edie. Riding in that car was like a dream.

Finally, though, the secret was out. We only lived thirty-some miles from Auburn, where they manufactured the beautiful and outstanding Auburn, Cord and Duesenberg automobiles. He worked at the plant. These cars he drove were what they called "demonstrators" and so he didn't own any of them. What a letdown.

One of Mary's suitors, and I think it was Dana Christner, once brought a whole box of candy bars. Babe Ruth bars, I think. Or maybe it was Milky Ways. Whichever, he didn't bring just one bar, but a whole box. My favorite, though, and hers too, was Truman Oesch. He had shiny white teeth and a friendly smile, always. He was a salesman and a good one. To be successful, a salesman needs to have a friendly personality and a sense of humor. He had both. One of the reasons he had such white teeth, I suspected, was that he chewed gum all the time.

I mean all the time. Commonly, the houses in those days had a special room called a parlor. You hardly ever hear the word any more unless it has to do with spiders and flies. One of the functions of a parlor was to receive young men coming "a courting."

Many's the time I used to shyly peek around the door leading into the parlor to ask a caller, "Got enny gum?"

This unwelcome intrusion into her privacy inspired my sister Mary to compose the following poem:

My Brother

My brother Ted is five years old
and a dear little fellow is he.
His eyes are blue, his hair is gold
and his cheeks are like apples to see.

It seems he's always full of glee
and when I'm in a pensive mood
It soon leaves when he's with me
and I cease to long for solitude.

Yes, my brother is a little dear
until my beau night comes.
Then, Oh! How embarrassing to hear,
"Hello there. Got enny gum? "

Then 'round the corner he will peek
and with a laugh and jeer
He reaches up with his little hands
and pulls my poor beau's ear.

I tell you it's humiliating.
He sure has lots of cheek.
When my beau's gone, he gets a raking.
Still 'round the corner he will peek.

But, boys will be boys.
We cannot change the fact.
And it does not mar my joy
if my beaux do not come back.

That's what big sisters are all about. In spite of my irreverent attitude toward her privacy, she still loved me. And, I love her, too.

Edie and girls from Vicksburg

6

The Strongest Man In The World

*M*y father was, without doubt, the strongest man in the world. Dad was born on a farm about a mile west of the "Black Walnut Farm." He was the oldest of seven children born to Fayette and Icy Woodworth. Grandma's parents lived on the "Black Walnut Farm" and owned at least one other farm. Great-grandpa's name was Jim Green. Never heard great-grandma's name. All I ever had to do was ask Dad, but I never did.

One of the biggest "shames" of my life is that I neglected to "pump" my grandparents about their experiences while growing up. My grandfather, Joe Todd, my mother's father, lived to 101 years and I could recount on one, maybe two pages, all the things he ever told me. Mainly because I didn't ask.

Come to think of it, Grandpa Todd did tell me something on a couple of occasions. Once, when I was four, he said, "Get out of my workshop, Teddy!" All I'd done was drive some staples into his workbench. But that's another story.

Another time, I think when he and Grandma were celebrating their 60th wedding anniversary, he said something like, "Get out of my house, Ted, and don't come back until you've learned how to vote 'right'." And that's another story.

Shucks! Look there! I hadn't intended to talk about that at all. What I intended was to insert a little blip, encouraging young'uns, and even those not so young, to talk *to your grandparents while you can*. Only in the New Kingdom will grandparents live forever. And even then, some of them won't.

Listen to what I say! Grandparents are like a good wife. Some of us don't appreciate them until they're gone. Enough! Let me get back to my story.

Dad was brought up in what is generally referred to as "The Old School." The thinking then was "Education beyond the eighth grade is a waste of time. Since you're going to be a farmer anyway, experience is the best teacher."

You're expected to live at home and work for your father, without pay, until you are 21. Maybe you get a little spending money, but during this time your father teaches you how to farm. When you turn 21, you may, if you wish, go out on your own. Of course, now if you can manage the time and decide to work some for neighbors or whatever is available, your wages go to daddy, if you are under 21. That meant there wasn't much money to spend and practically nothing to spend it on even if you had it. No television and not even any radio. Mostly just work.

But there was baseball or football, and, for the stronger young men, boxing or wrestling. More wrestling, really, than boxing. My dad was a good wrestler because he was strong. Farm boys worked hard.

Farm boys still work hard. Not just Dad but others have told me of his feats. Until. . . In his early 20's, Dad was injured playing football. Lots of pain. Unbearable pain. But nothing could be seen on the surface except that his leg turned black and blue. Dr. Schrock decided he had to go to the hospital in Fort Wayne. To make a long story short, they severed his sciatic nerve. Didn't mean to, but that's what happened. Doctors didn't then have the knowledge and expertise they have now.

Meanwhile, back at the farm. . .

But wait for another minute. I want to tell you what made me think of this story. Somebody has to jog my memory.

My wife, Zena, was telling me about this farmer in Smith County, Kansas, who was referred to affectionately as "Old Man" Teijan. His place was almost directly across the road from the Schoen farm.

Zena said he had never before owned an automobile, but one day he came home from Lebanon with a brand new Model T Ford. He parked it in the yard until he could decide where to keep it.

There was this sturdy metal building that he used for a tool shed. It had a door plenty big enough to let farm machinery in, so this looked like it would be perfect. Lots of room. About three times as deep as the car was long. After moving everything out of the way to make room, he started up the Model T and headed for the door of the "garage." With all the family watching admiringly, and the T Model moving at a pretty good clip, he suddenly realized he couldn't remember how to bring it to a halt. He started yelling "Whoa! Whoa!" But the car didn't come to a stop until he hit the end of the garage. Hard!

That wasn't the last time, either. Zena's dad, Herman Schoen, came back from the Teijan farm one day and nearly died laughing at how "Old Man" Teijan's garage was beginning to look like it was pregnant.

Well, Dad never had trouble like that. His problem was getting the T Model into the garage. As I've reported before, Dad's cars never had brakes and the clutch never functioned properly. So when we saw or heard him coming into the yard, there was a mad dash to help push the car into the garage.

There was a rather healthy incline up to the garage and a fair-sized bump where the door closed. So if he was going fast enough to get over the hump he would likely have hit the end of the garage like "Old Man" Teijan. On the other hand, too slow and he wouldn't get in the garage.

On this particular occasion, we were all working in the garden when Dad came home. We could see the dust cloud following him for quite a ways, so we had plenty of time to get into position.

Now I don't know what went wrong. Maybe everybody was worn out from working in the garden, but there wasn't enough "push" exerted to get the car into the garage. At some stage, brother Lloyd said, "Let it roll back and we'll give it another try."

Sure enough, I fell down. The car stopped. On me. Pandemonium reigned. Nobody seemed to know what to do. Except Dad. The Model T stalled and wasn't running. He jumped out of the car, took one quick look, and backing up to the left rear bumper he shouted instructions to my brothers, "When I lift it up, you pull Teddy out!" He lifted the car up and they pulled me out. Little or no harm done. Like I said, he was "The Strongest Man in the World." Anyway, I thought so.

7

A Sunk Sirted In My Eyes

"*E*die! Edie! A sunk sirted in my eyes. Will I go blind?"

No. He sure didn't. Matter of fact, when he was older, he could hit a fox squirrel in the left or right eye from a hundred yards with a .22 rifle. And he could find mushrooms while walking behind four other people who weren't finding any at all. But, that's another story. Let me go on with this one.

During the depression, our folks didn't have any more than enough money to buy groceries, let alone give money to young 'uns. Lots of others throughout the country were in the same boat.

So, Charles came up with the bright idea of becoming a trapper. Dad had some traps, so he loaned them to my brother. Said Charles could use his .22 rifle if he wanted, also.

Early one Saturday morning, Charles set out to establish a trap line. He was bundled up good and warm because northern Indiana can produce some downright cold weather in the dead of winter. It was almost dark when he got back to the house.

There was a slow-moving stream of water that I thought originated somewhere on the Wellington Bradley farm. It actually came from a lot farther away, but I had never explored for its origin. Anyway, it moved across our farm and into the woods. It was in the woods and along this stream that Charles set his traps. These were wicked-looking things that had to be forced open with your foot. The ones he had were called single spring steel traps. They had a chain on them about three feet long with a ring on the end of it. The ring was to drive a stake through to anchor the trap so an animal caught in the trap couldn't drag it away.

Usually, Charles would set his traps in the water hoping to catch a muskrat. They were the easiest fur bearing animal to find because they leave marked trails and live in dens. By setting the trap near the bank, just under the surface of the water and in the path they use, success is nearly assured.

Dad was the one who taught Charles how to trap. He was good at it himself, when he put his mind to it. Dad was good at a lot of things. When he set his mind to it.

Charles always ran his trap line early in the morning before going to school. Even on Sunday, he'd run his line before we left for Sunday School at the Bethel Church.

Everybody called the preacher "Reverend" Grantham. He was also a farmer. Edna Foltz and Vanus Miller played the piano on alternate Sundays. Both were real good. But, that's another story.

One day, Charles noticed a mound of freshly dug earth on a little ridge back in the woods. Looked like it might be a burrow. His inspection caused him to decide to set one of his traps alongside the mound.

The next day was a Saturday so Mom and Dad had gone into town. Mom to do her "trading" and Dad to "jaw" or play either rummy or euchre at Fisher's Pool Room. He was also better than average at billiards or rotation pool.

Anyways, Charles asked little brother Wayne to "help" him with his trap line. Charles was eight, at the time, and Wayne, six.

While I'm thinking about it, Wayne had a bit of a speech impediment when he was young, probably induced by big sisters, Edie and Mary, talking baby talk to him.

The boys checked several traps before they came to the mysterious mound where Charles had set the trap the day before. Immediately, it was obvious he had caught something. The dirt that had been almost neatly dug out of the hole was scattered every which way. No trap was to be seen anywhere. Whatever the critter was it had pulled the trap into the hole. But the stake, that had been driven through the ring on the chain and into the ground, had held.

Charles realized that whatever he had caught was still very much alive. Now, I'd be the last one to imply he knew exactly what he had caught but, the circumstantial evidence would indicate he did. "Wayne, I'm gonna need you to pull up on that chain. When his head comes out of the hole I'll shoot him with the rifle."

Evidently, Wayne didn't think too much of the idea because he argued that Charles should pull the animal out and Wayne shoot him. Charles explained that Dad had loaned him the rifle and he wouldn't want Wayne shooting it. So, good old trusting Wayne started pulling up on the chain. "He's 'tummin' out," Wayne said.

"Keep pullin' and I'll shoot as soon as I can see his head."

Only problem was, the trap had caught the critter by the hind leg and his rear end came out of the hole first. It was a skunk! It quickly cut loose with the only defense mechanism it had and squirted Wayne squarely in the face. In his eyes, his nose, his mouth, all over his face. Wayne let go of the chain. Fast. And the skunk went back into the burrow.

Wayne took off for the house running and crying and rubbing his eyes. All the way, he kept repeating over and over, "Edie! Edie! A sunk sirted in my eyes. Will I go blind?"

Edie not only heard but also smelled him before he got to the house. My sisters met him outside and while Edie guided him to the outdoor pump, Mary went back inside for a cake of soap. They cleaned him up as best they could, after stripping him down to the altogether, then putting clean dry clothes on him. Even though they left his clothes outside soaking in a bucket of soap and water, the house smelled of skunk all winter.

Moral? Never go into business with your relatives.

23

8

Blue Racers—Snakes, That Is

Déja vu (pronounced 'day zha vu'), a French word meaning, "the illusion of having already experienced the situation one is in for the first time." In my case, it had just been a very long time.

One day during our vacation to Indiana last summer, my wife, my grandson, Teddy, and I had spent 'til the middle of the afternoon at the Jacob Yoder farm helping thresh wheat. Didn't get there until about 11:00, so all I did was become re-acquainted with the sights and sound of a threshing machine in full operation. There's nothing in the world to compare.

The big diesel tractor that turns the belt operating the separator wasn't quite like the big steam engine Ed Miller had used. But that was over fifty years ago. The separator looked the same.

Two iron-wheeled wagons loaded with wheat bundles stood alongside the intake part of the threshing machine. As the bundles were fed in, care had to be exercised to keep from overloading the separator. Keep from bogging it down.

Ted had never experienced anything like this and wanted to see it all. Jacob took him "under his wing" and first thing you know, they were on top of the threshing machine. They were blowing the straw up into the barn. Alongside was a truck from the Lima Elevator loading wheat as it came out the chute. And, I promise you, it was really coming out. This particular field was yielding over eighty bushes to the acre.

After checking all of these things out, Ted wanted to help offload wheat bundles into the separator. He did good—as the feller says. Looked like a real pro.

Finally, everybody stopped for dinner.

A big wash tub of water had been sitting in the sun all morning. With the temperature over ninety degrees, the water was nice and warm by noon.

All the men tossed their straw hats on the lawn and gathered around to wash up. We shared communal water, soap and towel.

Sure seemed like old times. Then we sat on the lawn and talked until Jacob came and said it was time to come in for dinner.

"Déja vu."

There it was again. The big dinner table seating sixteen of us. Two at each end and six along each side. Just the men.

And food? Now my grandson, Ted, knew the meaning of "there's enough food on this table to feed a bunch of threshers."

It seemed like I had been there before.

After everybody had eaten their fill, they asked me to tell some stories. And I enjoyed doing that.

The story they enjoyed the most involved an incident that occurred the summer I was twelve. I was working for John C. Schrock. His farm was directly across the road from the Homer Mishler farm.

The main reason I was there was to help with chores and work in the fields. I wasn't big nor was I strong enough to do anything very heavy.

During my first few days at the farm, Mr. Schrock "taught me" to talk Dutch. He did it by telling me what different things were in Dutch. For instance, I remember the dog was a *hoont*. The dog's tail was the *hoont's schwanse*. The wagon was a *vogn-n-n*. You have to kind of hum the "*n*." Then the wagon's tongue was called the *vogn-n-n-n dikesel*. On the other hand, the tongue in your mouth was referred to as your *tsun-n-n-ng*. Seemed a little confusing to me.

Anyway, after three or four days, John said, "You've heard all the English you're going to hear. From now on you talk Dutch just like Polly and Mae and me." That was it! From then on all I heard was Dutch. But I lived. And I learned.

Sometimes I think maybe I learned only enough to get myself in trouble. Case in point:

One Sunday the Schrocks had company for dinner. City folks. From Sturgis, I think.

These were shirttail kinfolks who had been brought up talking Dutch but hadn't spoken it in some time. But they were this day. The mother was a real talker. I mean her mouth ran nonstop. Not only did she talk nonstop, but she gorged herself with Mrs. Schrock's delicious food at the same time.

During the dinner, Polly replenished the bowl of mashed potatoes. She handed them directly to this lady. In no time at all she had scooped a goodly portion onto her plate. They were hot! I mean, really hot. She quickly popped a big forkful into her mouth. Oh my! She choked and gagged and got red in the face. I thought her eyes would pop out. She grabbed her glass of water and started drinking.

"*Voss iss letts, Emma?*" John asked.

"*Ich gebrenn mine dikesel!*" she choked out.

I couldn't hold it! I busted out laughing. She had indeed burned her wagging tongue.

Pointing to the back door, Polly shouted to me, "*Ga! Und John, ga du mit!*"

I headed for the door, still laughing, with Mr. Schrock right behind me. I just knew he was going to thrash me, but he wanted out of the house so he could laugh, too.

Sometimes a sense of humor can get you in a mess of trouble. Enough! Back to work.

Riding the wagon to the wheat field with Andrew Yoder Jr. and his son Andrew Maynard, I was really struck with nostalgia. It had been fifty years since I'd helped load wheat bundles.

Junior gave me my choice. Drive the team, load bundles from the ground or load the wagon. I chose to load the wagon. Two quarts of perspiration and an hour or so later, we had it loaded and were headed back to the threshing machine. I felt tired, but fulfilled. It took a while for me to cool off. Then we drove to the Andrew Yoder farm.

After supper, most of us walked down the road to have a look at the "little grave." We were almost there when "deja vu" struck again. Byron Foltz, another guest, was walking in front of me.

When he kind of stepped sideways, a memory flashed before me. This was it:

My brothers invited me to play "follow the leader." Naturally, I was all in favor. They didn't often include me because I was "too little." Our "follow the leader" trek took us to this very spot in the road near the "little grave." At that time, the road wasn't much more than two deep ruts in the sand on this little hill.

I don't think Lloyd was with us, but Charles was in the lead and Wayne in front of me. We were all laughing and jumping as we followed the leader.

Then it happened! Wayne let out a piercing scream and, jumping to the side, he yelled, "Watch out for the snake!" There in the track in front of me was a snake that, at that instant, looked as big as a boa constrictor! I nearly died of fright. I turned and ran as fast as my legs would carry me, back to the safety of the house. Mom would save me, that was for sure.

My brothers had killed a big blue racer and had coiled him up in the road—just for my benefit. His head was pointed directly at me.

I'm still afraid of snakes.

9

The Day The Gypsies Came

*F*or what seemed like at least a year, we watched this building under construction. Nobody seemed to know what it was going to be. Caused a lot of speculation.

At first, we figured there was going to be another service station at this busy intersection. Yet, they hadn't dug any big holes in the ground for storage tanks. Finally, the framework indicated a big two-story building. Sure, we thought, probably a professional building of some sort. Doctors, maybe. Or a lawyer's office. One thing was certain, it was going to be expensive.

Before they put the two big ornate doors on the front entrance, we were able to watch as they built an open curved stairway to the second floor. The ceiling of the front room appears to extend to the top of the second floor.

Just before finishing the inside of the house, in the front room, they hung one of the biggest and most elaborate chandeliers it's ever been my pleasure to see. Extending almost the length of the front of the house is a huge portico. It will hold two large automobiles. With a little care in parking it would accommodate four.

This portico is supported by four huge columns on the outside and six against the house. It is most impressive.

Oh, yes! The exterior is light-colored brick and the wood trim is gleaming white. A high brick wall extends around three sides of the property and the front has a low brick wall with a white steel fence on top. Both entry ways have steel gates. Both driveways are red brick. The rest of the yard is grass and bushes, immaculately landscaped and kept.

But, no swimming pool.

And no garage!

Finally, it became obvious that it wasn't a business office. Just a private residence.

But, whose?

One day, unexpectedly, the mystery was solved. A call came from Randolph Jarrett, Jr., my adoptive grandson.

"Gramps! Gramps! Guess what? I met the man who owns the big house on the corner."

Before I go on with what else he said, I need to tell you a little about Randolph.

He's very excitable. Lots of nervous energy. Gets it from his mother, Marie, I think.

Among other abilities, he can run a mile without "breaking sweat." Has competed in marathons. His father, Randolph Sr., is also a runner. Now, I'm not saying "jogger." I'm saying "runner." Both keep very trim.

They're interesting people. Marie is one of those French-speaking beauties from the island of Martinique, while Randolph Sr. is from Panama, so he was brought up speaking Spanish. They married while both were attending medical school at the University of Mexico which is the largest university in the world. Both are now doctors of dentistry as were their fathers before them.

Randolph, Jr. broke with family tradition and entered the sales field. He is a dynamo with Copperfield, an exclusive importer of fine Italian men's wear. Randolph's early education was largely in Mexico. His command of English, Spanish and a smattering of French has been an invaluable asset in his sales career. Randolph was calling from Copperfields.

"Gramps! The man who owns the house just left here. He bought a 'slew' of clothes. He wasn't that easy to fit because he's only about 5'4" tall. I noticed his black wavy hair and black eyes. He has kind of an olive complexion."

Randolph stopped to take a deep breath.

"Anyway, he paid with cash. Over $800. Whoa! I thought. I've just got to know something more about this guy."

"While I was making out his sales receipt, I asked for his name and address. The man kind of objected until I explained that we like to have our better customers on a mailing list. The address he gave me I recognized as the big house on the corner. I wound up asking where he was from originally. That's when he told me that he was a Gypsy from Hungary."

"Gramps! They're Gypsies!"

Right off, I recognized yet another chance to have some fun with Randolph, so I said, "That explains why there's no garage with the house. They're nomads by nature and so can't bring themselves to see any need for a garage. That would also explain the huge chandelier. They have always liked big bonfires."

"Randolph," I said, "that reminds me of the day the Gypsies came when I was a kid."

"Some other time, Gramps. No time for a story. I've got customers. Call you later."

How times change.

We heard them singing as they passed our house. Happy, cheerful, free-sounding. As though they didn't have a care in the world.

It was a spectacular sight. Two sleek black horses, pulling a wagon with a house on it. Rectangular in shape. Probably about 6' x 1O' in length. With windows and curtains. The roof was kind of rounded. The horses wore shiny black harnesses and they had plumes on their heads like you'd expect to see at the circus. I'd never seen Gypsies before, except at Corn School. That was our County Fair.

These were men and women, all short. And such pretty clothes the women wore. Bright-colored scarves on their heads. Long purple, green, black or yellow dresses. Sandals. And jewelry! Long dangling earrings. Chains of glittery stones and silver around their necks and waists. You could hear as well as see their numerous bracelets jangling as they walked and sort of danced along. The men wore dark bell-bottom trousers, white shirts with puffed sleeves and flat black hats.

This was truly a sight to remember. It was more like a dream than reality.

Must have been a dozen of them. Most were walking, and coming behind was a man leading three horses. Dad said that most Gypsy men were horse traders and their women were fortune tellers.

They made camp about a quarter mile from our house. We could see them easily. After unharnessing the black horses, they staked them out with the other three a little further down the road so they could graze. Then they put up a tent. I was kind of disappointed because I thought they'd sleep out under the stars. Next they built a fire to cook their evening meal over and to see by. After they finished eating they really kept a big fire going.

Mom was up and down all night, checking on us kids. We were all worried about their being there because of stories we had heard about the things Gypsies do. No facts. Just rumors. But, that's what prejudice causes. Fear of the unknown. As the night wore on and until we fell asleep, we could hear them laughing and dancing and singing, accompanied by guitars and violins and what sounded like tambourines.

The next morning they were gone. They hadn't stolen any of us kids. Or anything else. I missed them, and everything seemed dull, after "the day the Gyspies came."

10

Presents from Uncle "Charlie"

*M*y grandfather, Fayette Woodworth, was not overjoyed when his only daughters were swept off their feet by a couple of country school teachers. He had wanted better for them. Aunt Beulah married Frank Carney. Aunt Mary became the bride of Charles Miller.

To be a country school teacher, at that time, did not require a college degree. A high school diploma was sufficient. Grandpa was a successful farmer, had some banking interests, and was involved in local politics. He didn't feel that school teachers had much of a future and he wanted nothing but the best for his daughters.

So it was, that Grandpa furnished them with the financial wherewithal, as well as the encouragement, to attend medical school. Dr. Frank Carney became a highly successful practitioner in St. Clair, Michigan. He was also, among other things, Mayor of St. Clair for over 25 years. Dr. "Charlie" Miller practiced medicine in Sturgis until his retirement. He and Aunt Mary had two children, Charles, Jr. and Ramona. When I was a kid, I had a real crush on Ramona. She was as beautiful as her name.

Although I saw them maybe once a year, I never got very well acquainted with Aunt Beulah and Uncle Frank. Probably, because they lived so very far away. St. Clair is only about 200 miles from LaGrange, but it might as well have been 2000.

Uncle "Charlie" and Aunt Mary used to visit us with some regularity. Every year they would come laden down with gifts for all of us. They were very kind and generous and it made them happy to see us so happy. Both of them had a good sense of humor. They laughed a lot and I liked that. Most of the gifts were clothing, but they were surely welcome. I was almost positive Uncle "Charlie" was Santa Claus without the red suit. I think Dad kind of resented Uncle "Charlie's" gifts even though we sorely needed them. There just never seemed to be enough money to buy necessities, let alone anything extra.

I can't remember what kind of car they drove when I was young, but in later years Uncle Frank drove a black Fleetwood Cadillac and Uncle "Charlie" a black Buick. They both looked right at home in these big automobiles which Dad called "Status Symbols."

One winter visit from Aunt Mary and Uncle "Charlie" stands out in my memory. My folks knew they were a comin', so they had "Killed the Old Red Rooster" and we had a merry feast of "Chicken and Dumplins. "A joyful time was had by all.

They plowed through some really big snow banks to get there and, when they finally made it, Dad was the one most surprised. He always said those big cars could never follow his Model "T" through snow drifts. This time, anyway, Uncle "Charlie" had made it.

Again, they had generously brought us gifts of clothing and toys. There were six of us kids and, somehow, they knew all our sizes from shirts to shoes. How happy we were and in fact, how fortunate we were. I've always thought Uncle "Charlie" was expressing his gratitude to Dad for helping put him through medical school.

I had the first tractor on our farm. Matter of fact, I had the only tractor that was ever on that farm. Long before Dad ever dreamed of owning a tractor, I had one. A toy. But, I had one. It was one of the toys they brought me. There was an accompanying wagon that hooked on a hitch on the back of the tractor. Combined, they were about 12 inches long.

Now, I had another use for the sand and dirt that I had so carefully sifted through a piece of wire door screen. I had put it in small bags and stored them in the well of the cellar window on the west side of the house. Snow and rain never got in the window, so they kept dry.

Although there never seemed to be any snow clear up to the house, there was invariably a snow drift running alongside the house for about four or five feet. This dry sand was excellent "gravel" for building roads along the side of the "mountain."

Many an hour I spent building roads and pushing my tractor and wagon over them.

I don't believe I thought so then, but maybe those were "The Good Old Days."

11

The Buzz Pile

*K*enneth Forgue owns this garage in Stafford called Precision Automotive. My daughter Edie and I have known Ken for quite some time. When we walked in on him the other day, Ken said, "It's too hot out today for man or beast. What kind of soda water do y'all want? I'm buying."

Edie answered him by saying, "What kind have you got?" She's not bashful.

Ken took his key out of his pocket and opened up the machine. "I've got Classic Coke and Diet Coke, orange and diet orange, root beer and diet root beer. Here's even a can down in the bottom, I don't know what it is." We made our choices and Ken got them for us. He picked out a diet drink for himself. He weighs about 280, I'd guess. Not fat. Just big.

When we went into the office, where it was cooler, Ken said, "Ted, you're always coming up with, 'That reminds me of a story.' Well, that odd-ball can of soda reminds me of a story. I listen to your stories, so you can just listen to one of mine for a change."

I thought that was fair, so I told him to "have at it."

"Last fall, some salesman talked me into buying a whole case of soda pop at a price I couldn't refuse. A few days later I took off for the lake to do some fishing. I iced this pop down and took it with me." Ken was beginning to warm to the story. "I've got some wooded lots on the lake and I decided to take along an axe and a chain saw so I could do some hackin' and choppin' and sawin' while I was there. Took my rifle with me, too. Might want to do some target practice." Lots of folks in Texas have a gun rack across the back window of their pickup truck. Mostly, there'll be a rifle on it. All the time. Day and night.

Ken continued, "Soon as I got there, I unloaded the truck. Then, I opened the cooler to sample my bargain. The salesman had said it had no caffeine, no sugar, and practically no calories. My first taste convinced me it also had no fizz, no taste and was no good, But, it came in handy. I used the full cans for target practice."

We thought it was a good story and laughed and started to leave. Ken said, "Hold on! I'm not finished. I've got to tell you about the dumb thing I did while I was hackin' and choppin' and sawin'." Edie and I both said, "Keep going," and he did.

"I had cut down some underbrush and piled it up and had a good fire going. I'd also sawed down some fairly small trees and piled them on the fire. But, there was this big tree that had a low limb on it I decided to cut off. It was probably 6 or 7 inches thick and was about 5 or 6 feet from the ground. I revved up the chain saw and started cutting away right next to the tree.

"I had one foot extended so that it was directly under the limb and the other one back about a foot. As the limb was about cut through, I moved my one foot further back, so I was leaning away from the limb. Unfortunately, I didn't move the other foot out of the way. The butt of the limb fell right on my foot.

"Have you ever done anything so dumb in your whole life? It mashed my foot good. Matter of fact, now, six months later, my big toe nail is just beginning to grow back."

He said the trip wasn't a complete waste, because he did catch a lot of fish.

Sure enough! His story reminded me of something that I did when I was five years old.

Dad had to cut a lot of wood to last through the long cold winters. Mostly, Lloyd helped him on the other end of a cross cut saw. They'd cut down a tree and then trim it. The limbs, big enough to cut up for firewood, were piled to the side and later hauled to the house on the bobsled. The main log would be too big to handle and they'd just cut it all up with the crosscut saw, right on the spot. This wood was hauled to the house when there was enough snow on the ground to use the horse-drawn bobsled.

All these limbs, when they were taken from the woods to the house, were put on the "buzz Pile." Dad had a big gasoline engine that turned the belt which operated the buzz saw. The engine had a big fly wheel on a shaft and the saw was made to turn the same way. When they were ready to start sawing the small logs—or limbs—into stove-length pieces, the boys would lift one up and put the big end on a saw buck. Dad operated this by pushing it toward the spinning buzz saw. It would quickly cut the log in two. Then the boys would move the log another "stove length" and again, Dad would push it against the saw blade. The blade turned all the time because there was no clutch on the gas engine. It was probably dangerous, but it sure was effective. They could saw up a big pile of wood in no time at all.

They'd never let me help. Said I was too little. One day, during the winter before I started to school, I decided to help in my own way.

They had spent a Saturday hauling logs to the house with intentions of sawing them up the next Saturday. There they lay, all week long, while Dad was in town and my brothers were in school. "Here's my chance," I thought. Although it was cold and there was quite a lot of snow on the ground, Mom had bundled me up and sent me out to play.

Dad kept all his small tools, including the axe, in the garage. It took me awhile to get the small garage door open, but I finally made it.

Taking the axe out to the buzz pile, I started hacking away.

Guess what? The axe came down on my right foot. It didn't seem to hurt all that much right away, but I could see that I had cut through the rubber on my boot. I didn't want Mom to see that, so I put the axe in the garage and went back out to see what else I could find to do.

Finally, I noticed that every other one of my tracks was all red. Oh! Oh! Fast as I could go, I ran for the house. "Mama! Mama! I cut myself."

I was pretty much covered with snow and still had my heavy outdoor clothes on, but she gave her entire attention to my cut foot. She unbuckled the boot and took it off. I could see the cut in the shoe, then. She carefully unlaced the shoe and took it off. It was a mess. Had a lot of blood in it. Then, she took off my sock. My foot was really bleeding because, you see, I had cut off my second toe. The axe had cut well back on my foot, too. Then Mom realized that even though the bone was completely severed, the toe was still attached by a thin piece of skin on the bottom.

While soaking my foot in cold water, to stop the bleeding, she took the rest of my clothes off. Then, with the help of a roll of gauze, she bound my second toe to the big toe and the third toe and then doused the bandage with iodine. Boy! Did that ever sting! The next step was to bandage the whole foot.

Then, the final step. Mom held me in her lap and rocked me like she used to do when I was little. But, I liked it.

Her home remedy worked. My toe is still there, turned kind of sideways and with a big scar, but it's still there.

Mother love is good medicine.

12

Ice Cream In Winter Time

*W*ouldn't it be nice if we could psyche ourselves to remember only the pleasant times of our past lives? I'm working on it, because I'm convinced that only morbid people get enjoyment out of hearing about another's difficulties or past problems. So, I'm going to strive to practice the philosophy, "If it wasn't a pleasant experience—forget it."

Different things will trigger my memory.

Couple of weeks ago my wife, Zena, pointed out an ad from the local chain store advertising ice cream, two half-gallons for $5. Then, the next day she handed me a short grocery list and asked if I'd mind picking up these few things. Included was two half-gallons of "diet" vanilla and a gallon of "two percent" milk.

Now, I sure wouldn't go broke if I bought the richer more expensive brand of ice cream and the milk with a half way decent amount of butterfat in it—but I bought what she asked for.

This reminded me of the story about the poor young man who scrimped his way through college by eating an inexpensive diet of crackers and skimmed milk. After he graduated from college and earned a lot of money, he developed an ulcer from so much worrying about his money. The doctor put him on a diet of nothing but crackers and skimmed milk.

The diet vanilla ice cream reminded me of the inexpensive way my mother used to make ice cream when I was a little "shaver." She'd send me out with a glass and instructions to pack it full with nice clean snow. While I was doing that, she'd pour about two thirds of a glass of milk and stir in a teaspoon of vanilla extract and some sugar. When I'd get back with the glass full of snow, she'd pour the milk and vanilla into it. To my young taste buds, that mixture tasted a lot better than this diet ice cream does to my much older taste buds.

One of the modern conveniences we had on the farm was an ice cream freezer. We didn't have a refrigerator or even an ice box, but we had an ice cream freezer. In order to be able to use this fine appliance, we had to have ice. So—it figures—we only had ice cream in the winter time. Even so, it couldn't have been called a regular occurrence. Most always, though, the first time would be the Saturday following the first really bad freeze of the winter.

One thing I remember, my sisters, Edie and Mary, would always see to it that we had a fun time. They made a veritable production of it. Ice cream was not all there was to it. Oh! No. Edie was the bestest devils food cake baker there ever was. Three layers and every layer covered with chocolate frosting. Mary's black walnut fudge was so rich and smooth it melted in your mouth. Between the fudge and the cake, I'm gaining weight just thinking about it.

But, in order to "bring this thing off," there had to be walnuts cracked and ice brought up from the pond. Somehow, after each "cracking," whatever it was for, there were never any nut meats left over for the next time they were needed. They just didn't "keep" with six kids in the house.

Cutting the ice out of the pond was quite a trick. Naturally, the ice had to be frozen solid enough so it could withstand being walked on. When a nice clean spot of ice was found, Lloyd or Charles would hack a small hole in the ice with a hatchet. Then with a hand saw, they'd cut out blocks of ice about twelve inches square. These would be put in a gunny sack to be carried to the house. Placing the sack on a flat hard surface, the ice was crushed by hitting it repeatedly with the flat side of an axe.

Mom always mixed the ice cream. Now, you notice I said, "ice cream?" I didn't say, "ice milk" and for sure I didn't say "ice skim milk." She made ice "cream." I remember. She made it with cream, eggs, sugar and vanilla. I can remember her opening and putting in a can of peaches sometimes. Mostly when she made vanilla, she'd add a cupful of chopped walnuts. It sure was good.

After pouring the ice cream mixture into the can and putting the beater inside, it's time to put the top on with its gears and crank. After turning the crank a couple of times to make sure the gears are going to mesh, it's time to start adding the ice. While one person adds the ice, another turns the crank. After about two or three inches of ice then it's time to add salt to the ice. Then more ice, etc. Ice cream will not freeze if there isn't enough salt added to the ice. On at least one occasion, I remember Charles getting the blame for forgetting the salt. The ice cream wouldn't freeze. Once the oversight was discovered, salt was added and in no time —ice cream!

As if ice cream, devils food cake and candy wasn't enough, the chances were pretty good that the girls would make a big dishpan full of popcorn. Sometimes the popcorn was saved until last and we ate it as we sat around the table playing a card game called "Rook." The rules of the game couldn't have been very difficult to master because I was allowed to play, too.

The part I remember with the most pleasure was that everybody would be in a good mood and enjoying themselves. We laughed and we talked to each other. Somehow, I can't recall our doing that very often. How sad.

Like as not after all this joyful family fraternizing, Dad would suggest that we "retire" to the parlor and maybe Mom would entertain us by playing the old reed organ. Grandpa Todd had bought it for her when she was just a little girl. All of us would stand around the organ with arms intertwined, singing while Mom pumped and played. We sang right well, if I do say so.

Lloyd is the only one still singing—to amount to anything. But the old reed organ still plays beautifully. I know that for a fact. It sits in my parlor, now.

13

The Old Reed Organ

*M*y wife doesn't have very many hobbies. Unless you count playing the "old reed organ," making baby quilts, or baking bread.

Zena does all three too infrequently. She plays the organ when the mood strikes her, and that's not very often. She makes quilts for our special friends when they have a baby. And, when I put on enough pressure, she bakes better bread than any of my family ever thought of baking.

Not that my mother couldn't bake good bread—not that my sisters can't bake good bread—they can . . . .

Aw, shucks! By now, you can tell I suffer from a severe, incurable, case of "foot in mouth" disease.

Maybe—just maybe—if my wife baked bread with more regularity I wouldn't think it was so great. But, I doubt it.

And her quilts? Not more than a month ago a husky young man walked up to us and said, looking at my wife, "You don't know me," and we didn't, "but, you made my 'security blanket.' I love you for it and I'll never forget you. 'Bye." And he walked away. We still don't know who he was. But, it sure made my wife feel good. She puts a lot of love and effort into making those "security blankets."

Recently, on one of those rare occasions when she took a notion to play the organ, Zena was giving her rendition of one of my favorites, "Drink To Me Only With Thine Eyes." I love it. And it has a nostalgic effect.

That organ has entertained a great many people. Mostly in Mom's family. It is also known as a "Crown" organ.

Grandfather Joe Todd bought the organ from the George P. Bent Mfg. Co., Chicago, Ill., and gave it to Mom when she was only nine or ten years old. Sylvia Pearl Todd, that's my mom, had a musical ear—or an ear for music—even when she was a young girl. She sang well and accompanied herself on the organ.

Grandpa Todd let Mom take the organ with her when she married my Dad, Ira Cecil Woodworth.

Dad never much cared for the name Ira, so he always went by the name of Cecil. Signed his name Cecil Woodworth. Not many people ever knew his name was Ira. I guess it's not important, now.

My most vivid memories of the old organ would have to be the times when Dad and all six of us children would gather around Mom as she played the organ in the evening. It really seemed to bring us closer together. Dad sang baritone, Mom sang alto, and as near as I can remember the kids all sang soprano. I just know we sounded good. Some of the songs I remember were:

"Old Folks at Home"

"I'll Take You Home Again, Kathleen"

"In the Evening by the Moonlight"

"Those Endearing Young Charms"

"When You and I were Young, Maggie"

And, the one we all thought was great, "She'll Be Comin' 'Round the Mountain When She Comes." We learned every verse and there must have been a dozen or more. There was "She'll be ridin' ten white horses when she comes" clear on down to "She'll be walkin' 'round the mountain—"

And then, "We'll kill the old red rooster—" And on and on.

A very fond memory.

I mustn't forget "In the Garden" and others. Hymns sound better when they are played on an organ than on a piano.

Not many pieces of furniture followed us on the different moves we made after we left the farm, but the "old reed organ" was one that survived them all. But, over years, the organ fell into disrepair. Mom had pumped on the two pedals so much the carpet was not only completely gone, but the wood was mostly worn away by her shoes. Some of the fancy dowels were broken and a number of the "stops" were missing. The upper part of the organ was removed and stored in the attic in the house in town. For a short period of time the roof leaked. The silver on the back of the mirror became bubbly. Some of the beautiful carving was destroyed. The bellows were going bad and mice had gotten into the reeds. The organ wheezed more than it played.

In about 1963, when I was visiting the folks, Mom offered to let me have the "old reed organ" if I would buy her a new water heater. Theirs had gone on the "fritz." Sounded like a good idea to me, so I arranged for a company in Sturgis to ship it to Houston. I had it sent directly to the Thomas Goggins Piano Co. When they had taken it apart enough to determine the condition of the playing mechanism, they dropped the "bomb shell." To recondition, repair, replace parts and refinish the "old reed organ" would run about ten times its original cost. I nearly had a stroke of apoplexy. But, I let them do it and I wouldn't take ten times that for it now.

Most people who enter our home will stop to look at the organ and say, "How lovely. Do you play?" Zena can say, yes, but my answer has to be, no. Mom taught my sisters to play, but none of us boys.

In the winter of 1980, my niece, Phyllis, and her husband, Cleo Hartzler, spent a few days with us. We took a leisurely trip to Matamoros, Mexico, where we enjoyed, among other things, the Mexican food. Frijoles, tacos, chalupas, chili con queso, tortillas, frog legs, guacamole salad, cabrito, membrillo, cerveza—you name it—we tried it. "Tequila?" you ask. Gee! I don't seem to remember. But, the real joy was the association with loved ones. It can't be beat.

A memorable occasion while they were here was the night my daughter, Edie, and her husband Bill, and their two kiddos, Tabetha and Timothy, joined us. We wound up standing around the organ with Phyllis playing and the rest of us either singing or playing one of the musical instruments Mom had given me. The sweet potato, the kazoo, the tambourine, the harmonica—Mom played them all.

She was a remarkable woman, my mother. I can't look at the "old reed organ" without thinking of Mom. And, I still miss her.

14

Get Out of That Cherry Tree, Charles!

*I*t's a fact that every story has a moral. True, some are not easy to detect, but finding this one will be as easy as falling out of a tree.

All three of my brothers were climbers. There were no mountains nor even any hills on our farm, so they had to climb whatever was handy.

The strawstack was one of their favorites. You know. Pretend it's a mountain. Dad never fenced the cows and horses away from the strawstack, so it never took long before all the straw around the outside was either eaten or tramped down until the strawstack looked like a giant toadstool. It wasn't all that easy to climb onto the stack then, but they could do it.

They would climb in the barn, all around the rafters. You should have seen them go hand over hand all the way across the barn hanging from the hay loft track. Sometimes they'd go all the way across playing "follow the leader", other times they'd drop—one at a time or all at once—onto the hay below. All of this was accompanied by lots of screaming and hollering and laughter.

Then there were trees and we had lots of them. This story involves my brother Charles, when he was six years old, and a big cherry tree that stood only a few yards from the back door of our house. It was a red cherry tree. You know. The sour ones used for baking those scrumptious pies.

The timing of this episode was in the spring, just as the cherries were beginning to ripen in the top of the tree. That's the way it works. If they are exposed to the direct sun rays they ripen faster.

Anyway, Charles was way up in the top of the tree picking and eating some of the tree's "first fruits" when Mom caught him. She was coming out the back door wiping her hands on her apron

45

when she spotted him up there—precariously perched on the highest limb that would hold him. She literally shrieked at him. "Charles! Charles! Get down out of that tree before you fall and break your arm!"

No, Charles wasn't really a disobedient boy, just mischievous. He knew Mom wasn't about to climb the tree to make him get down, so he decided to play the moment for all it was worth. He broke off a little limb with several reasonably ripe cherries on it and threw it down to her. "I'm not going to fall, Mom. Here, I'm throwing you some cherries."

"No, I don't want any cherries. I just want you down from there before you fall and break your arm."

Still baiting Mom, he reached out as far as he could and called down, "See, Mom, I'm all right. I won't fall." But, Mother had prophesied correctly. He did fall and he did break his arm. The limb broke and down he came, clawing and grabbing at limbs all the way down. It might not have hurt him at all, but his arm was kind of twisted under him when he hit the ground, kerplunk.

All of the screams and cries from both Charles and Mom attracted the attention of Uncle Bela Woodworth who was horseback riding only a couple of hundred yards away. He was across the road in one of the back fields of "The Black Walnut Farm." I am told, and I'm sure it must be true, that Uncle Bela's big black horse leaped the fence as they charged across the field and into the yard to see what had happened.

It was obvious that Charles's arm was broken. Dad wasn't at home, so it was agreed that Uncle Bela would take Charles to LaGrange on his horse and that's what he did. Mom bandaged his arm and made a crude sling and away they went. Uncle Bela took him to "Old" Dr. Schrock's office and he "set" Charles' arm. "Young" Dr. Schrock, Stewart, I think has name was, had died a few years back.

News travels fast in a small town and it didn't take long for Dad to find out what had happened. He came to the doctor's office and then took Charles home in the car. Dad wasn't happy. He lectured Charles all the way home about the dangers of climbing. But, that's not the end of the story.

46

As spring ended and summer wore on, the broken arm was knitting very nicely. It had slowed Charles down. A little. Just before time for school to start in the fall, catastrophe struck again. Arm out of the sling, Charles was rolling an old Model T tire on top of the long chicken house. It had a corrugated metal roof which gave off a nice rumbling sound to the rolling tire.

Through the back window, Mom saw him. Practically flying, she rushed out the back door shouting, "Charles! Charles! Get off that roof before you fall and break your arm again." She startled him and sure enough, it took his mind off what he was doing just long enough that he, and the tire, went plunging off the end of the chicken house. He landed on a horse drawn mower standing alongside.

Can you guess what happened? No. You're wrong. It was worse. He not only broke his good arm, he also re-broke the other one. When Dad brought him home this time, he had both arms in a sling.

The silver lining in this dark cloud was that now Charles wouldn't be able to start the first grade.

The worst indignity of it all was that, without the use of his arms, he couldn't feed himself, so sisters Edie and Mary were assigned to see that he got fed. He nearly starved before he'd open his mouth so they could feed him. They'd say, "Open your beak, little birdie" and then laugh. They were getting even for some of the pranks he had played on them.

Moral? Obey your mama!

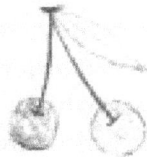

15

Helling Potatoes

*I*t was around the summer of 1930 that my brother Lloyd raised an acre of potatoes for his FFA project. Lloyd might argue that it wasn't 1930, but the date isn't important. One thing I remember for sure is that I was just a little kid and didn't get in on much of the "fun."

Lloyd and all the rest of my brothers and sisters attended Shipshewana High School. Me? I graduated from LaGrange High School. Never did go to "Shipshe," as they called it.

The town of Shipshewana has a lot of interesting history. It was named after an Indian Chief and, as a matter of fact, there is an impressive tombstone marking the site of his burial alongside Shipshewana Lake.

Anyway, Riley Case was the principal at the high school, as well as the coach. In addition, he was head of the agriculture department.

Lloyd was a first string basketball player and, like all farm boys, took agriculture.

In whatever year this happened, I do remember that there was little market for potatoes at digging time. Something had to be done.

Mr. Case said it would be good if we could keep the potatoes in limbo until the middle of winter, maybe February or March. That posed a problem in that we had no place to store such a big stack of potatoes to keep them from freezing. Dad came up with the solution.

"We'll 'Hell' them," he said. "We'll dig a big hole on that ridge in the field west of the house. All we need to do is line it with straw, put the potatoes in, cover them with more straw and then cover them over with dirt. They'll keep 'til late winter or until the market improves."

And that's what they did.

Mom objected to the use of the term "helling" potatoes, but Dad told her it was once in common usage, merely meaning to put into a pit. He said there were other meanings for 'hell' than "the bad place."

Dad read a lot and he used to enjoy looking up the meaning of different words in an old Webster's dictionary. It's dated 1847. 1 know it is, because I still have it.

In the Old English dialect, the expression 'Helling Potatoes' meant not to roast them (as one might think, if you put them in Hell) but, simply, to place the potatoes in the ground or in a cellar.

That might not sound like a big project when I say, "They dug a hole and put the potatoes in it and then covered it over." But, considering that they did it all with hand shovels, without the aid of even a horse drawn scoop, it was a big job, to say the least.

I can't recall how many bushels of potatoes they had, but my memory says they completely filled the big truck my bother-in-law, Truman Oesch, had pressed into service to haul them to Chicago. He drove the same truck that he used to sell and deliver feed from. His brother Dan, who owned the Topeka Roller Mills, had given him permission for this extra-curricular activity.

Last week I bought three pounds of potatoes for a dollar. They were on special. I thought it was a good price. Lloyd would have been tickled to death to have gotten a dollar for three bushels. Times change, don't they?

Dad was always one to "kill two birds with one stone" whenever the opportunity presented itself. Let me tell you how he did it this time.

Close by the spot where they dug the pit to bury the potatoes was an old orchard. There weren't many trees left, but they produced excellent, though unusual, apples. One was called Northern Spy. Dad was especially partial to them. Seems as though they ripened in the summer, some time after Harvest apples were ripened and gone. Their consistency was such that they wouldn't lend themselves to being shipped all over the country. For this reason, I wouldn't be at all surprised if they have been allowed to become extinct.

That would be a pity.

Russet apples were the other ones I wanted to mention. Their skin was kind of rough, rather than nice and smooth, and they looked like a yellow apple that had gotten rusty. Now, it really wouldn't surprise me if those apples had been allowed to die out. Why?

Everybody knows that peaches or pears, plums or apricots—you name it—always taste better when they are allowed to ripen on the tree. Same thing applies to apples. But, Russet apples? You could let them hang on the tree until snow fell and they just would not ripen.

The only way to ripen a Russet apple is to bury it. And that's what Pa did. He and my brothers picked every last apple off those trees and buried them with the potatoes.

And there Dad was with another silver lining. Although they got virtually nothing for the potatoes, we surely had some tasty apples for the rest of the winter.

16

Taking Direct Action

My mother-in-law was a woman who believed in taking direct action. She was a fine lady and a tower of strength to her husband and eight children, even though she was barely five feet tall. Her name was Esther (Nead) Schoen. There are a number of Neads in the Goshen area and many Schoen descendants in Elkhart and throughout Kansas. Mama Schoen had sugar diabetes and died in 1945 at age fifty-one. Some day I'll write a story just about her. But, for now, let me tell you of one experience we shared.

Zena had talked me into going to Kansas to meet her family. None of them had been able to come to our wedding, although shortly thereafter, Mama Schoen had traveled by train, and by herself, to meet the man who had swept her beautiful daughter off her feet. Direct action, like I said.

Mama was disappointed in me and said so. Again, direct action. "You're not a man. Just a tall skinny boy and I'm going to call you 'Teddy Boy.'" And she did. Always.

One day, while we were in Kansas, she asked Zena and me to go to Lebanon with her and Ethyle Belle, Zena's youngest sister. We jumped at the chance and she let me drive. They had a 1937 Ford.

While we were in Lebanon it started to rain. Mama told me to take the car to a garage and have them put the chains on the tires. I thought she'd jumped her trolley. It was the middle of summer. Before I could put up much of an argument, Zena told me, real serious, "You'd better do as she says."

When I found the garage, I had to get in line. Others were having their chains put on, too.

After Mama had finished her shopping and Zena had talked to, minimum, a dozen of her old friends that she hadn't seen for over a year, we headed back to the farm.

For the first few miles, we were on a well maintained gravel road. As we approached the dirt road where we had to turn off, Mama started saying, "Slow down, Teddy Boy! You're going too fast!" I was slowed down to only about ten miles an hour and couldn't imagine what she was getting all excited about. "Slow down, Teddy Boy! You're still going too fast! Slow down!"

As I turned off the gravel road, I abruptly knew what she was talking about, The car started sliding side ways, piling up mud as we slid. It didn't seem to be slowing us down much.

There was a creek flowing, at this point, alongside the road. I promise you, there was a very sharp ten foot drop off to the bed of this creek.

We were turning to the right and sliding to the left. So, Mama was on the right side of the car. Before I realized what was going on and just how much danger we were in, she had the right door open and she was standing up. Ready to jump. Taking direct action. We stopped sliding. She didn't have to jump. But, we were right on the edge with about three yards of mud between us and the sheer drop off.

I can't describe the rest of the trip. If you've never experienced Kansas mud, you wouldn't believe it anyway. But, for the record, it's slicker than axle grease.

Her taking direct action reminded me of something my dad did one time. Mom used to try hard to get us to the Bethel Church every Sunday. Mostly, Dad didn't go and so Mom drove. Mom was a good driver except Dad thought she drove too fast. But then, he thought any speed over twenty five miles an hour was too fast.

The road that we lived on was just one lane. As a matter of fact, most of it could have been described as being two tracks. Grass grew in the middle of the road. It took some first class maneuvering to pass an oncoming vehicle.

There was more than one obstacle to keep us from going to church. One was the humongous mulberry tree hanging out over the road at the corner where we turned toward Palmer Hill. Mom usually manipulated the Model "T" around it going "to" but coming "from" was another matter.

More than once she wound up in the ditch, trying to avoid the branches of the mulberry tree. This Sunday found us in the ditch again, partly because it had been raining and the road was kind of slick.

When we finally got out, all of us were covered with mud, including Mom. It never fazed Mom very much so we were laughing when we drove into the yard at home. Dad didn't think it was funny. Taking direct action, he said, "I declare! I'm going to put a quietus to this business of having to dodge that blasted tree." And he did.

After they had changed clothes, Lloyd, Charles and Wayne loaded into the car with Dad—along with his double-bitted axe and the crosscut saw.

Mom tried to get them to at least eat dinner before they left, but they were gone. Edie and Mary helped Mom fix something extra, because it was for certain they'd be starved when they got back. Nearly two hours later, they showed up. Hungry as a bunch of bears.

Dad said, "The tree's gone. We not only cut it down but we sawed it up in stove lengths. As soon as we finish eating we're going to hitch up Barney and Prince and haul the wood to the house. You see, Sylvia, there's some good in everything." Yep! Dad could find the silver lining in any dark cloud—if he set his mind to it.

17

The Butter Churn

"*P*rocrastinate," Webster's Dictionary says: to postpone or defer taking action; to delay. "Woodworth's" Dictionary says: to put off until tomorrow something you should do today.

I ought to know because I'm an expert. Been doing it for years. Right now, just looking around me, at least a dozen things either need to be painted, washed, cleaned, put in a frame, hung up, put up, or thrown out. Not to mention repaired, replaced or finished.

If my wife and I ever had a garage—or yard—sale, and displayed everything we have that we don't need, everybody stopping or passing by would think we were breaking up housekeeping, for sure.

"We're going to have to get rid of that" is one of our most common sayings. The answer is usually, "No, surely somebody can find a use for it." Old habits are hard to break.

There's no two ways about it, I had a good teacher. My dad. Now, he was a procrastinator "of the first water," as the feller says. There wasn't anything he couldn't find a way to postpone.

When Mom would complain about big holes in the back screen door, Dad would tell her that the little holes were to keep out house flies and the big holes were to keep out butter flies. Then he'd laugh. Mom never thought it was funny. After a couple of weeks he'd come home with a roll of wire screen.

For one reason or another it would be another two or three weeks before he'd replace the old screen. Nearly always, something kept him from plowing up a garden for Mom as early in the spring as she wanted. We lost a lot of tomatoes that way, because a large percentage of them had not yet ripened when the first heavy frost came.

As a general rule, we didn't have a good supply of firewood laid by when winter came. As a result, we often burned wood that had not been given time to dry and age properly. It surely did not produce the maximum of heat, either.

Procrastination has a habit of causing more problems than it ever solves. Dad meant well and so do I. Tomorrow, I'm going to start doing better.

"Somnambulism." Webster says, simply, "sleepwalking." Somewhere I read that a person is most likely to sleepwalk during a period of worry or tension. It also said sleepwalking occurs more commonly among children than among adults. Most sleepwalking is harmless. But a sleepwalker may injure himself by falling out a window or down stairs or by walking into an obstacle.

Now, I don't always agree with everything I read—even when an expert is being quoted—but in this case, I'll go along with what they said. Especially with the "during a period of tension or worry." There's one thing I'd like to add: "Sleepwalking may be caused by an attack of bad conscience."

No matter how you look at it, it's plain to see that somnambulism has the potential for causing a lot of problems. Let me tell you of a good example.

My grandmother Todd had a wooden butter churn. Probably was about a five-gallon capacity. It operated very simply in that a lid covered the top and a rod ran down through this. Attached to the rod were a pair of thin boards about two inches wide, forming a cross. By a handle attached to the top of the rod, you raised this cross, or "X" up and down, agitating the slightly soured cream, until it turned to butter.

Dad had bought Mom a "modern" churn. It was made of glass. Only about two and a half gallons in capacity. This churn had kind of a gear box on top with a crank on the side to operate it. Inside was an affair that looked kind of like the blades in an ice cream freezer. Matter of fact, it worked pretty much the same except you could see through the glass. You could actually watch the cream turning to butter.

Came the day when Mom made butter, there were lots of helping hands because this was an occasion. We thought it was entertainment at its best. And we loved the butter.

Churning butter was not the usual thing at our house. More likely we had oleomargarine, not a pleasant memory to me.

After this one particular churning, when everything was cleaned up, I was told by Mom to take the new churn down to the basement and put it on the shelf where it was normally stored. I procrastinated! Instead of taking it to the basement, I opened the cellar door and put the churn on the first step, intending to take it on down later. You see, Dad had brought home groceries, including a lard boat of bulk peanut butter, and for the first time in a long time we were going to have fresh bread and freshly churned butter and, my favorite, peanut butter. I didn't want anything to delay this "happening."

This was one time that realization exceeded expectation. I hadn't been able to imagine how good the bread, butter and peanut butter were going to taste. It was truly delicious. But, I completely forgot about the butter churn.

Some time after midnight, I got out of bed and walked down stairs. The bedroom I shared with my brothers was on the second floor. I wasn't aware of doing this because I was walking in my sleep. I had walked in my sleep before. But this time, it was because of a guilty conscience.

The stairway to the basement was directly behind the one leading to the second floor. Actually, the upstairs stairway formed the ceiling for the basement stairway.

When I finally quit wandering around and started to go back upstairs, I opened the basement door instead of the upstairs door. Rather than the step going up, it went down—and so did I! And, so did the glass butter churn!

What a racket! It woke everybody in the house. The bottom landing was made of stone and when the churn landed, it smashed into a thousand pieces and me right on top of it. Such a scream as I let out you never heard.

Mom got there first. Mothers always react in emergency situations faster than anybody else. I was hurt. Bad. My left hand was cut severely. Lots of lesser cuts. Mom bandaged me up and doused the cut with iodine. It healed.

Procrastination and somnambulism didn't kill me, but it sure slowed me down. The moral to this story is: Keep a clean conscience and don't put off 'til tomorrow anything you can do today.

18

Grandma's Buckwheat Pancakes

"*W*e're going to Grandma's house" have always been words welcomed by little kiddos the world over. There's something magical about it. Grandma's are special people to little ones. For some unknown reason, her cookies are better—and there seems to be more of them. Her house seems warmer in the winter time. She laughs more and she'll listen to you. Mothers don't always have time to listen.

Not all Grandmas are the same.

My Grandma Woodworth was always very formal. For instance, you were expected to knock on the door before coming in. Why, she even sometimes kept the doors locked! Since she lived real close to us, on the Black Walnut Farm, we got to see her with some regularity. I often used to stop there on my way home from school. She may have been formal, but she kept cookies on hand and she loved me. I loved her, too.

Now, with Grandma Todd, there was no formality. And no locked doors. She even seemed about half irritated if you knocked and made her come to open the door. She always greeted us with a big hug and a "Why didn't you come right on in?"

Grandma and Grandpa had a 160-acre farm east of LaGrange and a little south of US 20. They lived on the same farm for at least forty years.

All during the time Grandfather farmed, he worked as a painter in his free time. Not a painter—like in "artist," but painter like in— he painted houses and barns or inside walls. You know what I mean.

Grandpa taught both his sons to paint. Uncle Henry made his living painting for most of his life. Uncle Lewis preferred being a farmer.

Once my folks let me spend a whole week with Grandma and Grandpa Todd. I learned more about them in that week than I did all the rest of the time they lived—and they lived a long time. They had been married 75 years when Grandma died at 95 years of age. Grandpa lived on to 101. Neither died a natural death. Grandma died of cancer—and that's not natural—and Grandpa choked to death on a piece of meat. A Heimlich maneuver would have saved him, for he was in good health—all things considered.

Anyway, back to the week I spent with them.

In a way, I thought they acted like a couple of big kids. They loved to listen to the radio. There wasn't any TV then and even radio was kind of crude by today's standards.

Some of the programs they listened to were "Jack Armstrong, the All-American Boy," advertising Wheaties, "The Breakfast of Champions." Then there was "Little Orphan Annie" and I don't remember what she advertised. There was "The Great Gildersleeve" and "Fibber McGee and Mollie." I mustn't forget "Amos 'n' Andy,"

"Lum and Abner,"

"Little Jimmy" and several more.

This was their entertainment. There wasn't any other. I doubt they ever saw a movie or a stage play. Maybe, but I doubt it.

One day, after having helped her churn butter, Grandma gave me a glass of fresh buttermilk. Since I always tried to be respectful to my elders, I reached for the glass when she handed it to me, even though I didn't care for the taste of buttermilk.

That night—and every night—after the supper dishes were washed and dried and put away, Grandma started preparing breakfast. She could do that even while listening to the radio.

It must have been that Dad didn't care all that much for buckwheat pancakes, because I don't remember our having them at home. White flour and corn flour pancakes, yes. Buckwheat? No.

Grandma and Grandpa didn't feel as though they had eaten a proper breakfast unless it included buckwheat pancakes, and that's what she started preparing nearly every night. She mixed up the batter, including yeast, in a big pan and set it on the floor behind the pot-bellied heating stove and left it overnight. Self-rising buckwheat.

She made it all from scratch. Could have been there was a "starter" involved, but I can't remember. Probably was.

The next morning the batter looked like a huge loaf of bread. Grandma started working with it about the time she figured Grandpa would be finished feeding the livestock and milking the cows. It seemed as though the pan of batter diminished some in size as she stirred it.

While thick slabs of smoked ham simmered in a skillet on a back plate of the big wood burning kitchen stove, Grandma baked pancakes. Great stacks of pancakes. In order to keep them hot as she baked more, they were put on a big plate in the warmer.

At the first sound of Grandpa coming in the back door, Grandma would start breaking eggs and putting them in a frying pan. Six of them. Two for each of us. The big foaming buckets of milk Grandpa had carried in didn't get separated until he had eaten a hearty breakfast.

After he washed his hands and face, Grandpa was ready to eat. "Well, Teddy, I'm about starved. How about you?"

"I was beginning to think you'd never finish chores. Everything smells so good I can hardly wait."

"Well, why didn't you come on out and help me then?"

Grandma got into the conversation. "Joe, let the boy alone. Besides, he was helping me. Weren't you Teddy?"

"Sure was, Grandpa. I set the table."

Finally, we sat down together at the breakfast table. Not only did everything smell good, but it looked good. And, in short order, we were finding out that everything tasted good, too.

Grandma and Grandpa had coffee while I had "sweet milk." That's fresh, whole milk. Don't think we'd heard much about pasteurization at that time.

I ate like there was no tomorrow. Made a real "pig" of myself.

First, two big pancakes. Then gobs of fresh churned butter. On top of that came hot, thick brown sugar syrup.

After I'd eaten half of the two pancakes, Grandma put a slice of ham on my plate and then two eggs on top of the ham.

Every morning! The same thing! About the only deviation in the breakfast menu was the occasional substitution of thick slices of smoked bacon for the ham. Equally delicious!

No doubt Grandma Todd fixed an exceptional dinner and supper as well, but it is the breakfast that stands out in my memory. She was one fine cook!

I wouldn't have minded a bit if Grandma had asked Mom to let me stay there permanently. But, she didn't ask, and it's just as well—Mom wouldn't have let me, anyway.

19

One-armed Huckster

*G*eorge Thanos is one of the last men I can remember who truly made a concentrated effort to stand behind the slogan of the company he represented. It was, "Trust your car to the man who wears the star."

Two others who felt the same way were Demos Thanos, George's son and Evangelos Balias, George's son-in-law. They too "wore the star."

I mention George Thanos because it was at his station, while I was making a sales call, that I was approached by a legless man in a wheelchair. In his lap was some sort of a machine.

His comment to me was brief and to the point. "Pardon me, sir. Would you like to have your Social Security card in bronze?"

My mind flipped back to one of my earliest remembrances, Dad showing me a picture hanging on the wall of Dunten and Norris' hardware store, I think it was. The picture showed a tall thin man with a cane in each hand. Protruding to the ground beneath his pants legs were the bottom ends of his wooden legs. The caption beneath the picture read, "I complained because I had no shoes until I saw a man who had no feet."

Without hesitation, I let him make a metal copy of my Social Security card. I paid what he asked and gave him some extra. He expressed genuine gratitude, shook my hand and said, "God bless you."

Co-incidentally, shortly thereafter while I was making a call on a big tire store, something similar happened.

The Knapp Shoe Company has salesmen call on industrial plants and on businesses. They sell steel-toed shoes, dress shoes, or whatever you need. Now, you have to wait for your shoes because the salesman just takes your order. The shoes come to you later, by mail.

As it happened, the employees at the tire company didn't order anything.

As he was leaving, I walked up to the salesman and introduced myself. He set his satchel on the ground and extending his left hand he said, "I'm Paul Naylor, the Knapp man. Would you be interested in buying some shoes?"

I didn't especially need them, but I bought a pair of heavy-soled (oil resistant) work shoes and a pair of dress shoes.

The reason he shook hands with his left hand was—well—it was the only one he had. The right hand had very recently been severed at the wrist. I could tell it was just barely healed.

While he was writing up the order, I couldn't help but note his poor penmanship. He was holding or balancing the order pad on his right arm while writing with his left hand. Just sure he had a sense of humor, I said, "You're not left-handed, are you?"

His answer was, "Yes, I am, but not by choice." And he laughed.

We both felt no need to pursue the subject.

Out in California, there's a fellow I know who lost the use of his legs in a serious automobile accident. His name is Tim Reese. His mom and dad, Mary and Dave Reese, own an auto parts distributing company.

Within months of his realizing he'd never walk again, Tim was "up and at 'em," taking over the operation of the company's computer system, from his wheel chair.

Through a lot of prayer to his God, Jehovah, as well as encouragement and support from his parents and many friends, Tim has been able to "carry his own load" in many ways.

When I was a kid, the "Raleigh Man" used to come to the farm once a month. He had a big territory and he kept busy at it. His name was Ernie Yoder. It was a treat to have him come by. He seemed a very quiet person and we thought of him as company. We didn't get much of that. He drove a covered truck that we would now call a step-van. You could walk right in and look at the merchandise on the shelves. Most of what he had were spices or extracts for the "buttry."

Mom called the little storage room off the kitchen the "pantry." Dad said it was the "buttry." I think he got that word from Grandma. Boys tend to cling to things their mothers teach them.

The Raleigh man had a lot of things on his truck that were not "Raleigh" products. He had bottle openers, can openers, soap products, brooms, buckets and small cooking utensils. If he didn't have what you wanted, he would get it. He believed very strongly in the old adage, "You can't do business from an empty wagon."

If you didn't have the cash to pay for what you needed, he wasn't averse to bartering. Mom once wanted some fruit jar openers he had. They worked like a charm. Mr. Yoder let Mom try one out on a jar of peaches from the year before. It had one of the zinc lids with a rubber ring seal. Those are virtually impossible to get off without some sort of assistance. She was able to get the lid off with ease by using the fruit jar opener. I don't remember what they cost, but Mom traded him an eight-pound barred rock hen for them.

Oh! I almost forgot. Dad called him, respectfully, "The one-armed huckster." You see, he had only one arm.

Another man I knew in my younger years was "Pete" Weirich. His family lived a little way from the "six-mile curve."

"Pete" had an accident and lost a leg while he was hitching a ride on a freight train. (There are those who would say he was a "Bum," but he wasn't. "Hobo," maybe. "Bum," no.) He was an honest man out of work, but he was looking for work. Any kind. Just like a lot of men during those depression years.

When I knew him, he wore a peg leg, but he was working at a service station at the six-mile curve. The station was owned by a man whose last name was Nelson. But, "Pete" was working. Like all those other men I've mentioned, he was working.

You know? Dad just might have taken me to see the picture of the man who had no feet because I had complained about his putting cardboard in my shoes. The soles had worn through so there were holes in both shoes—and I only had the one pair.

It's a good lesson to learn. No matter how bad our situation might be, there's always somebody who is having more and bigger problems than we've ever imagined. "You'll never see the light at the end of the tunnel unless you keep your chin up and your eyes looking forward."

An old Woodworth truism.

20

Hauling Gravel For The County

*M*y dad helped in the construction of U.S. Highway 20. That was always hard for me to believe because I couldn't remember when it wasn't there. It is a known fact that children resist the idea of change. The road was a good example. When I was a child, I was just sure that Highway 20 had always been—and would always be. Not so. My Dad had helped build it. It hadn't always been.

For that matter, my Dad helped build the Old Valley Line Railroad and it was already out of service by the time I started to school. The railroad ties and tracks were still there, but abandoned. They ran right in front of the County Farm.

Dad got what was considered good pay in those days. The U.S. government paid the wages for workers on U.S. 20. He had to furnish his own team of horses and he was paid $3 for a ten-hour day. The Valley Line Railroad was a private line and only paid $2 a day for a man and his team.

Along with roads "always having been and always being," there are parents. Young children just can not conceive of their parents ever having been little children. Nor can they comprehend the idea of parents ever growing old. But, they do.

Maintenance of the road in front of our farm was the responsibility of the county. Since paved roads were virtually nonexistent in the county when I was a wee tad, the county highway department had its hands full. And, since there were only two farm houses on our road, you can well understand that ours was not a "top priority."

We were generally the last ones to see the snow plows after a heavy storm, also.

Finally, county commissioner Frank McCauley got tired of Dad's complaining and he said, "Cecil, we just don't have the manpower or equipment to take care of the lesser traveled roads. Why don't you take care of it yourself?"

"Well, in the first place, Frank, I don't have a gravel bed for my wagon and in the second place, it's your job to see that the road's maintained, not mine." Dad told him right off.

"How about if the county paid you?" Frank asked.

"Now, that would throw a different light on the subject. What's your proposition?" Dad wanted to know.

"If you'll build yourself a gravel bed that will haul three cubic yards of gravel, we'll do some business together."

"Where's this gravel supposed to come from?" Dad asked.

"There's a gravel pit back in the woods at the Latta farm the county's been using for your area. It's the first farm west of Ed Miller's, so it's about two miles from your house."

After some negotiating, Dad agreed to a contract to haul gravel for the county for a dollar a load. It turned out to be one of the hardest contracts Dad ever tried to fulfill. First off, he had to get the needed two by fours and two by twelves from the Farver Lumber Company. They cost him as much as he got for the first, I don't know how many, loads of gravel he hauled.

In the summer, all four of us boys would go along to the gravel pit to help Dad. I doubt I was much help, but I went along. Actually, it was quite an adventure for all of us. We spent a lot of what is now referred to as "quality" time together.

Dad told us stories of things that happened to him when he was a kid. We really enjoyed them even though it seemed somehow he always wound up telling us how hard he used to have to work for his father. Without any set pay.

The lane that led from the road back to the gravel pit ran alongside a long stretch of some kind of fir trees. They had been set out some years before and there must have been four or five trees wide. Being where they were made them a good windbreak for the farm buildings in the winter time.

It was a fair distance from the road back to the gravel pit. Once we got there, we all discovered there isn't any easy way to load gravel with a shovel. It isn't like loading sand or even plain dirt. Gravel has lots of stones in it. Makes it hard to shovel.

Barney and Prince were not too pleased with this job. Not only was the gravel heavy, but the wagon was run right into the pit. This meant the wagon was in loose gravel and would always settle down some, making it seem even heavier. They always got out, though. Barney and Prince were good horses and worked well together.

On the way back to dump the gravel, we'd ride on top and entertain ourselves by throwing rocks at posts or whatever likely target presented itself.

We'd also pretend the yellow stones we found in the gravel were gold and save them in a can. We'd take it back to the house with us.

At first, we unloaded the gravel at the spots in the road that needed immediate attention.

Dad would stop the team so the wagon was directly over a bad hole in the road. The two by fours in the floor were loose, so all we had to do was keep working with one until it could be turned sideways and the gravel would start to run out. Once we'd get one turned, the others were much easier.

When the road wasn't real bad, the gravel that dropped down was exactly the right amount for that space. The length of the wagon was how much gravel we spread each day. By the time Barney and Prince were hitched up in the morning, driven to the gravel pit, the wagon loaded, back to the road in front of our farm, load of gravel dumped, there was not enough daylight left to go back for another load.

So it figures. We were hauling gravel for the county for one dollar a day.

Those were the "Good Old Days"?

21

Fire at the Gushwa Farm

*W*hen the giant, bright red fire trucks go roaring down the street, my heart seems to stand still. An emotion that is impossible to describe tends to take control of my very being.

If I am close enough to see the firemen, their expressions are always the same. The driver and his passenger, as well as the three standing on the back of the truck—all the same. It is one of concern. Of intensity. Or "Let's hurry. Time's 'awasting."

The fire truck itself adds to the feeling of urgency. Nothing can quite compare with the sight and sound of a diesel-powered fire engine speeding through heavy traffic with red lights flashing and siren screaming.

Worry, fear, anxiety are my first thoughts.

Then, hope. Yes, even a quick prayer. "Please, God. Don't let anybody get hurt." Seems like I heard Dad say that one time.

When I was a little kid, up until the time I was about six years old, I slept in a trundle bed in my parents' bed room. Dad never liked that arrangement very much. Maybe that's why I never used to know when he came to bed. He always waited until I was fast asleep.

On the other hand, he read a lot. He enjoyed reading the Bible or a newspaper. And with a fair amount of regularity, Dad used to read the "Monkey Ward" and "Rears and Sawbuck" catalogues. And dream. That could have been the reason he never went to bed especially early.

On this particular late summer night, Shep was raising a real genuine ruckus. I say genuine because Shep used to bark at about anything. Dad used to claim, unfairly, that Shep slept all day and barked all night. This night, though, his bark was serious. "Wake up!" he was saying—or barking. "Wake up! Something's wrong!" You know what I mean. A real urgency.

Well, I never knew if Dad was just coming to bed or if Shep had woke him up. All I knew was that a feeling of great excitement filled the air. I think Dad was trying to keep me from waking up—without success. Too much noise. Too much "electricity" in the air.

Dad was standing at the south window with Mom, looking out, and all my brothers and sisters were clustered behind them. There was a great glow on the horizon almost as though the sun was rising in the south. In the south? Couldn't be. Dad was saying, "It's Charlie Gushwa's farm, I'm sure. Either his house or maybe the barn is on fire." That's when he said, "Please, dear God. Don't let any of them be harmed."

Must have worked. Nobody was harmed. Then he said, "We'd better get over there and see if there's any way we can help. Lloyd, put your clothes on while I get the car started. You're going with me. Now, hurry!" In just a few minutes they were gone.

Dad took two milk buckets and two shovels with him. I can guess what he vaguely thought he might be able to use the pails for, but I don't know what he intended to do with the shovels.

The Gushwa farm was about a mile southwest, as the crow flies. More like two miles by the road. From our house, the fire made a huge glow in the sky. It was not a still night and as the wind would move back and forth the glow would likewise move from east to west and back again. Never before had we seen anything like it and I for one, didn't feel as though I ever wanted to see it again. To say the least, it was a traumatic experience, watching somebody's barn burn clear to the ground, even from a distance.

Mom kept trying to get us to go back to bed. Without success. She couldn't sleep, either. We were all just too wide awake to even think about sleep.

As the night wore on, the fire was finally subdued. There was no longer an orange glow in the sky. At about this same time, the wind shifted so that we could smell the fire. Again, something really different.

Dad and Lloyd finally came home. "Dragged home" would be more like it. Boy! Were they ever dirty! Black from head to toe. And, smelling of fire.

They told us some of what had happened. None of Charlie's horses or cows were in the barn, but some hogs were trapped inside. They died. He said a lot of men showed up to help. They managed to save at least some of the farm machinery. Neither the house nor any other buildings caught fire.

Mom made Dad and Lloyd take a good bath and she put their stinky clothes to soak. Only then did we all go to bed for a few hours.

Dad drove all of us over the next afternoon to see the damage. The barn was still smoldering. There were still fire trucks there, just in case it flared up again. The smoldering was coming from a large bin of oats. I'll never forget the pungent odor. It was new to me. And, that wasn't all. The barn had been literally packed with hay. It, too, was still smoking.

Since there were no fire hydrants to draw water from the fire trucks were more like tank trucks. Had their own limited water supply. They kind of let the fire burn itself out because of a lack of water.

It was assumed, as was generally the case, the fire had started by spontaneous combustion in the hay mow. This is usually caused by putting hay in the mow before it is dry.

A while back, my brother Charles and I stopped at the old Gushwa farm. Byron Foltz lives there now and has owned it for some time. He and his family had lived on the farm east of us at the time of the fire.

After visiting and reminiscing for some time, I asked Byron if he remembered when Charlie Gushwa's barn burned.

"Do I remember? I think of it almost every day. Let me show you something." With that, he led us out in the yard where he showed us a good part of the old foundation of that same barn.

Some memories have tangible reminders.

Edie Hewgley

22

Eating Mushrooms, Raw!

*D*ad taught us to hunt mushrooms almost as soon as we were able to walk. We loved them—fried—with beef steak. Dee-e-e-licious. They had to be fried—preferably in butter. Nobody ever heard of eating them raw, and never heard of them being raised commercially, either.

When I saw a picture recently of Kenny Myers holding up a 10-inch, five-ounce mushroom he found in the woods near Mongo, I did a double take. For one thing, I used to know an auctioneer name of Kenny Myers. This wasn't him. Too young.

Another thing, the mushroom was even bigger than the ones my brothers used to find—and they found some big ones. Wayne, especially. Maybe it was because he went hunting them more often than the rest of us.

For one thing, he used a different system than we did. Wayne was 6'3" tall and had long legs, giving him a longer stride. Because of that, he was able to cover a bigger area than most anybody else. We tended to walk slowly and almost stare at small areas where we felt sure there would be mushrooms. Wayne, on the other hand, kept on the move, sweeping a wider area with his glance.

I've always maintained that Wayne had better eyes than we did. Do you suppose the incident with a skunk—the time he got squirted in the eyes—might have given him super-human eyesight? Naaaaah! I doubt it. Wayne liked to hunt and eat mushrooms so much that when the season in northern Indiana began to come to an end, he'd go further north to Michigan. Around Cadillac, mostly. Rarely did he bring back less than a bushel of them.

Dad was no slouch as a mushroom hunter either. He taught us kids. Now, I know for a fact there are thousands of different kinds of mushrooms and many of them are edible. On the other hand, there are some highly poisonous varieties. No cure. If you eat one, you're dead. Dad led us to believe, for our own good, there were mushrooms and then there were toadstools. Mushrooms were good to eat and all toadstools were poisonous. That's not necessarily factual, according to the experts, but it's probably the best course.

The only mushrooms he allowed us to pick were what I now know to be the "morel." The body or cup looks like a cone-shaped sponge, pitted like a honey comb. Kind of brownish tan in color, completely hollow.

Now that I think of it, we used to call them mushroons. Pronounced *mush-er-runes.* That's Hoosier dialect. Took me years to break the habit. Probably never would have if my daughter Edie, hadn't pressed me so much. Said it sounded "uneducated." She can pronounce "mushroom" correctly, but she never was much good at finding them.

In the meantime—back at the farm—we had some company from Vicksburg. This would have been May, probably 1929 or 1930. Stanley Hackett and two lady friends came to visit. My sisters, Edie and Mary, were about the same age as they were. Stan was related, in some way, to my Grandpa Todd. Mom said he was our cousin—4 or 5 times removed. Anyway, they wanted to see the farm. It was an experience for them. Everything was new. Seemed like they asked a hundred questions.

The day before, my brothers had gathered a good mess of mushrooms and we had already eaten them when this unexpected company arrived. After being told about it, Stan said "I want to see where you found them. Maybe I can find some, too." Back to the woods we headed. All of us, except Mom and Dad. Stan and the girls were dressed in their Sunday best. Stan wore a suit and necktie and the girls had on real pretty dresses. One was wearing a tight fitting hat, which was the style. I remember, because I have pictures.

Picture-taking was not a common occurrence at our house 60 years ago. For that reason, I felt downright special when one of the girls wanted her picture taken with me.

Truly, they made me feel special. Even though I was way the youngest and we were brought up to believe children should be seen and not heard, they talked to me. And—they listened when I talked to them.

They seemed interested when I was able to point out that some of the trees were beginning to bud out. The girls were delighted when I showed them clusters of wild Sweet Williams and violets as beautiful as only wild flowers can be. Then, there were daisies and other flowers I can't remember the names of. One plant that couldn't very well be called a flower was called "Jack-in-the-box." Unusual, to say the least. Mayapple "umbrellas" seemed to be everywhere. Dogwood trees were in bloom as well as wild apple. It was a beautiful time to walk through the woods.

But, wait! Stan found a mushroom! He actually found one.

After being told that it was indeed an edible sponge mushroom, he picked it. Holding it by the stem, he kept turning it round and round in his hand and smelling of it. It wasn't a very big one, really. Suddenly he popped it into his mouth and ate it. Raw! We'd never heard of such a thing. Imagine. Eating a mushroom, raw!

All the rest of the afternoon we watched Stan, expecting him to keel over—poisoned—at any time. But, he didn't. If anything, it seemed to give him more energy.

Finally, it was time for them to leave. We had very much enjoyed their visit. We never saw them again.

Rumor was that Stan met an untimely death. Dad said one of the girls probably "done him in." Dad said it wasn't smart for a young man to date more than one girl. And—never—never—two at the same time. Dad used to give some real good advice—and I miss him.

23

Husking Black Walnuts

*O*ne of my earliest and fondest memories of Indiana is black walnuts. Now that I live in the South, they are just that—a memory. Did you know that black walnuts—or for that matter white walnuts—don't grow in the South? They only grow in what is known as the Temperate Zone.

Many people in the South have never heard of black walnuts. They don't know what they've missed. As a rule, though, when you mention that some of the most expensive pieces of furniture as well as gun stocks are made of walnut, it rings a bell. But, not the nuts.

White walnuts are more often referred to as butternuts. The nut is longer and the husk is not so thick. The husk just kind of dries up and so doesn't have to be removed. The nut meats of butternuts are sweet and ever so tasty. They surely do enhance the taste of chocolate fudge.

In the fall of the year, after it had frosted, you could always tell which of the school kids had walnut trees at home. Their hands would mysteriously turn brown.

We used to believe that Indians covered themselves with the juice from walnut husks. That's how they got their color. It wasn't so, of course.

There were lots of walnut trees in our big woods. We used to spend a "goodeal" of time gathering walnuts, according to Dad. After it had frosted, my brothers would climb the trees and shake or stomp the limbs until all the walnuts had fallen. Their husks were green, so the ground looked like it was covered with green baseballs. Then they were tossed into several piles to be put in burlap bags. That's when the fun began.

Lloyd would bring Barney, our favorite horse, back into the woods. He would patiently stand there while the boys loaded bags of walnuts on his back. They would sort of "scrooch" the bags around on Barney's back until they had molded to all the ridges, then they'd head for the house. Barney seemed to step almost gingerly to keep the bags from falling off.

Back at the house, the bags were emptied as soon as possible. Close proximity with other walnuts will cause the husks to turn black and for some unknown reason, maggots will tend to infest them. Keeping them separated, it almost never happened.

One of the simplest ways to get the husk off was to put the walnut on a hard surface and hit it, not too hard, with a hammer. The husk will separate and you can pick the nut out and throw it in the basket. Picking the walnut out of the husk with your bare hand is how the juice gets on you and turns your hands very dark brown. Another way is to simply step on them. That'll do it, if you're heavy enough.

Dad had a real nice corn sheller with a wooden frame and cover. Even the legs were wooden. Two big rough iron wheels inside turned in opposite directions. The big hand-operated crank on the outside activated the gears that turned the wheels. The ear of corn went in one side and directly into the space between the wheels. The shelled corn dropped through the bottom into a bucket and the wheels forced the cob on out the other end. Presto! Chicken feed. And—dry corn cobs to start the fire in the kitchen range. When Dad wasn't home, the boys used the corn sheller to very effectively husk walnuts. It worked like a charm.

Before I forget it, there was an absolutely enormous walnut tree that stood right along the road by the driveway in our front yard. It had to have been well over a hundred feet tall. In addition to producing many bushels of walnuts, its luxuriant foliage provided shade for most of the front yard.

The boys discovered early on that any walnuts that fell in the road or in the driveway were husked by the cars running over them. All they had to do was pick up the walnuts. Maybe that's where Dad got the idea of using the Model "T" to husk walnuts. He had Lloyd jack up one of the back wheels of the car after they had built a trough to put under it. He slightly inclined the trough so the walnuts would roll under the wheel as he "fed" the trough. He then cranked the car and let it idle.

That one wheel turned even though the car wasn't in gear. As Lloyd fed them in, the turning wheel just sort of sprayed walnut, husk and all, out the back side. All Charles and Wayne had to do was pick up the walnuts and put them in a basket. Admittedly, I can not convey, in writing, the excitement we all felt watching the wheel spit the walnuts out the back. The next step was the drying process. Nothing very elaborate. We had a very long chicken house. The roof was corrugated, galvanized tin and it sloped only toward the rear. The boys would put a 2x4, or any other boards that were handy, across the lowest part of the roof in order to keep the walnuts from rolling off. Then they'd put the walnuts on the roof to dry. The sun took charge of that. The drying, that is. It never hurt the walnuts to be rained on. Matter of fact, it cleaned them. After the nuts were completely dried, they were again bagged and stored in the basement.

Cracking walnuts and listening to Mom play the reed organ was one of the ways we spent many a long winter evening.

24

Let's Play "Zippy"

*T*he kids in my neighborhood fare right well when it comes to toys. The kids under five have toy cars and trucks as well as games and puzzles and construction kits. And stuffed animals? Listen! If they don't each have over ten, I'll be surprised. All different kinds and sizes. But, always a favorite one. That one will have a name. They love it like it was a real person. Sort of a security blanket, I guess.

When they're old enough, or big enough, to reach the pedals, their parents buy them either a tricycle or one of those plastic three wheelers call "Big Wheels." These things make enough racket to drive any adult out of their head. But, the kids love them. Virtually every one over five, boy or girl, has a two wheeler. They do things with them that I would never have thought possible when I was young. I never had a bicycle myself, but those who did were never able to do a "wheelie."

When we lived in LaGrange, our neighbor, Charlie Marchand, used to be able to ride a bicycle while he was sitting backwards on the seat. None of us kids were ever able to do it. We thought he was really something and he entertained us often.

Skateboards? The things they do with skateboards are almost unbelievable. Sometimes you'd think the board was glued to the boys' shoes, the way they jump curbs and over obstacles.

Most of the boys who don't skateboard have a scooter. These are something to see. Fancy! Rubber tires that have to be pumped up. A hand brake. This is a lever that sticks out of the handlebars. They're painted all different colors and have pictures of different creatures painted on them. Very elaborate.

There are at least five Go-Carts in our neighborhood. Two just plain stripped down Go-Carts, one replica of a Model "T" Ford, a Pennzoil Formula racer and a replica of a Mighty Distributing van.

Still, mothers hear the lament, "I don't have a thing to play with," or "There's nothing to do."

The other day I was watching a re-run of "The Rifleman" on TV when I noticed a street scene in which a boy was rolling a steel hoop with a stick. It brought back memories.

My brothers were real first-class innovators when it came to finding something to do. Rolling hoops was one of them. But they didn't need "The Rifleman" to show them how to do it. They managed to come up with different-sized hoops and even some wheels that could be pushed with a stick. Charles went one step further. Somewhere, he came across some pieces of plaster lath. He took a one-foot piece and nailed it across the end of a four-foot piece, forming a "T". It was a whole lot easier to push a hoop with this "T", especially a small hoop.

I'd hate to try to guess how many miles we rolled rubber tires. This was mostly follow the leader who tried to find paths that would be hard to follow. I was always last.

There weren't many trees that my brothers didn't climb. They sure did get plenty of exercise. I wasn't much good at climbing, but I tried. They spent a lot of time climbing in the barn, too. There wasn't a foot of climbable space in the barn they didn't cover, walking on the rafters or going hand over hand all the way across the barn on the hay track. They were strong.

Mom used to buy big cans of hominy from the IGA. We liked the hominy, but the cans came in handy, too. Another toy. My brothers would set them on top of fence posts and then throw rocks at them. When I played, they let me stand closer to give me a better chance of hitting the cans.

More than once, we would kick one of these cans, first one brother then the other, all the way to school. Lots more fun than just walking.

Beyond a doubt, the game they invented that gave us the most entertainment was "Zippy." Nothing to buy. All you needed was an old broom stick. First, you sawed the broom and all that wire off. Next, you cut a piece about eight or nine inches long. You needed a long piece, too. Actually, that's all the equipment you needed. Two pieces of broom stick. Next, you dug a small trench in the ground about 12 inches long and about three or four inches deep. I nearly forgot. In order to play this game, you need a playing field about half the size of a baseball diamond.

The rules of play are not complicated at all. The player with the long stick was called the batter. The other players were all fielders. They all stood out some ten to twenty yards from the batter.

The short stick was laid across the small trench, sideways. The batter would then put the long stick in the trench and quickly flip the short stick as far as he could in the direction of the fielders. They were supposed to try to catch it.

If the stick was caught, the one catching it became the batter. If it wasn't caught then one of the players threw it back to the batter. He was still at bat.

This time, instead of flipping the short stick toward the other players, he hit it toward them with the long stick. Again, if nobody caught it, he was still at bat.

The next time, he had to tap the stick into the air and then hit it out. If nobody caught it this time, his at bat consisted of tapping it into the air not just once, but twice and then hitting it out. The next time, three, and so on.

There seemed to be no end to the games my brothers could invent in order to amuse us all. But, for a fact, I don't remember my brothers ever having any store bought toys. Maybe they did have—but I don't remember any.

25

Raccoons

*H*ardly anybody calls a raccoon a raccoon. They use the word "coon" for short. There are lots of them in Indiana. As a matter of fact, coons can be found most anywhere from South Canada to South America.

A full grown coon can weigh 25 to 30 pounds and measure as much as 36 inches in length from its nose to the end of its tail.

Except for its feet and lower legs, the raccoon is covered with long, coarse hair that is grayish in color, with black tips. The underfur is pale brown. Its tail is bushy, grayish-white, with black rings. The face looks like a fox with a pointed nose.

As far as looks are concerned, the thing that really stands out is the black patch around each eye and the ring of white hair around it. This gives the appearance of a burglar's mask. It truly fits a coon's mischievous nature.

Their favorite foods are frogs, crayfish, snails, turtles, and other freshwater animals. They are fond of all berries and other fruits. And corn? They eat it so greedily they can ruin a corn crop with their visits. Before or after it ripens! Makes them no never mind.

Raccoons have long legs and strong claws. Their hands or paws rival those of a monkey. They have no problem opening a hooked gate or even twisting a door knob until the door opens.

One way they maintain their considerable strength is by climbing trees, which they do when pursued or hunted by coon dogs. They live in hollow trees whenever possible.

They enjoy the water and like to paddle in it. Many coons can whip dogs twice their size—especially in water.

Mother coon teaches discipline the old fashioned way, with a stern paw, and will attack and fight ferociously if anything threatens her young.

Perhaps their worst faults are robbing birds' nests and raiding chicken coops.

Many years ago, coonskin caps, sleigh robes and overcoats were popular. Today, raccoon coats for women are made from the original long-haired pelt, or the hairs are plucked out, leaving the pale brown underfur. This is called "sheared raccoon." No two ways about it, the fur coat is beautiful.

Dad gave his whole-hearted support to Charles and Wayne when they told him of their plan to trap coons. Not only was there a good market for their pelts, but every year, regular as clockwork, they would attack the corn field, en masse. To at least thin them out seemed like an excellent idea.

During the late fall and winter, Charles would put a dozen or so ears of corn in a pile and then set steel traps all around. He'd put it close to the stream, because coons like to dip their food in water if they can. They probably aren't really washing it, as it would appear, because they don't seem to care if the water is clear or muddy. They'll dip anything, even a frog or a small fish, before they eat it. Now, it wouldn't seem as though they'd need to be washed. Would it?

Charles was not overly successful. Many times the coons would figure out a way to snap a couple of the traps, then they'd walk right over them to get to the corn. More than once, they'd push the corn onto the other traps and spring them. It appeared as though they had done it deliberately. A coon is really wise. Lots of instinct. Yet we call them "dumb animals." Now, I'll not say they never caught one, but their failure rate was much higher than their successes.

On rare occasions, Dad would go coon hunting with some of his friends. "His friends from town," Mom used to call them. Dad had a lot of trouble walking any appreciable distance, so he didn't go often. Seems to me as though he used to go with Otis and Cobby Van Wagner. The names of Basil and Hansel Wallace pop into my mind, too.

We never were allowed to go along, but Dad used to tell us about it. The other fellers always had real long flash-lights that would make a thin, bright light clear to the top of the highest tree.

Some, but not all, would carry a rifle. Most of them had coon dogs. They all felt like it was just about the best sport imaginable, to go coon hunting on a moonlit night.

The dogs made the kind of sound only a coon dog can make. And, when they had "treed" a coon, you could hear their barking and baying for miles, on a clear night. Dad said when they shined the flashlights up in the tree you could see the shining eyes of the coon, but you couldn't always see the coon itself.

After a lot of "milling" around under the tree, the excitement of the chase would kind of wear off. In actuality, the chase was the big thing. Nobody wanted to shoot the coon very bad, and that was the only way to get him out of the tree. They'd excuse themselves by claiming the rifle hole would ruin the pelt. Dad and his friends never hunted coon for the meat, although roast coon is considered a delicacy in the South. Like I said, the big thing was the chase.

Isn't that the way it is with a good many other things in life? There's an old saying, "Anticipation is better than realization." Ain't it the truth?

Dad told us about another old coon hunter saying, attributed to "Hill-Billies," that went like this:

> "Ye kin haive muh waf er muh mule,
> but iffn ye tetch muh haown dawg,
> yer daid!"

I never believed that.

26

Cat Language

*M*y brother Wayne talked cat language, and very convincingly.

We always had several mousers—er—cats on the farm. They "mewed" in different tempos and pitches. Wayne said they were talking and he was able to interpret their "speech" for those of us who didn't understand cat language.

They did the majority of their talking at milking time, it seemed. Mostly they'd says such things as, "Koy-blar, tin I hass a dwink of milk?"

"Koy-blar" was cat talk for "Lloyd." The cats had different—and interesting—names for all of us. For instance, sister Edie was "Keedy-blar." Mary was "Canary Kanute." Brother Charles was supposed to answer to "Chab-lar." Wayne said his name was "Kame-lar," according to the cats. And I was "Keb-lar."

The cats didn't talk to me very much because I didn't milk the cows. I think the cats talked to Wayne the most, because if one of them mewed—or said—or whatever, "Kame-lar, tin I hass some milk," he'd always spray milk at them. The cars were real good at catching a stream of milk. They'd hold their mouth open and even move their heads to follow the stream. Hardly spilled a drop. Dad never cared much for this game my brothers played. "Wasted milk," he said.

During a recent visit to the farm where I was born, I was reminded of the cats that seemed always to be present some 60 years ago when I lived there. While I was sitting on a step watching little Becky Yoder milk a cow, I was playing with a tabby cat, listening to it purr. Becky said, "That's a mama cat. She had some kittens a short while ago. One of them got stepped on."

"Did it die?" I asked. "No. My uncle told me to give it two aspirin and let him know in the morning how it was. It got well." Becky's only six and as cute as a "bug's ear." She kept on milking all the while she was telling the story. Never missed a stroke. The foam kept rising.

Her big sister Ruth was milking on the left side. Becky was on the right. My grandson, Ted Hewgley, was milking (for the first time) the cow next to them. His partner was Adam Yoder, who's about Ted's age. That was something to see. Then there was Andrew III and his mom, Rose, on the next one.

As I recall, Andrew Sr. was milking one by himself, I asked him, "How come they're milking from both sides? I've always been taught you'd get kicked if you milked from the left side."

"If you start a cow out that way, they don't know any different. Besides, I've always felt they give more milk if you milk from both sides at the same time." Who am I to argue with a professional?

There were other things different, too. Instead of using one-legged milk stools they used stools made with three pieces of two by fours nailed together to form a two-legged stool. Then there was a little piece of carpet tacked on the seat.

A sort of a flat platform was placed under the cow's udder to set the milk pail on.

There was little chance of the cow kicking the pail over, because each cow being milked had very sturdy kickers on. (I don't know why they aren't called "kick preventers" or "anti-kickers," but they're called "kickers.") These were made of two pieces of metal about two inches wide and shaped to fit the back of the cow's hind legs. A chain tightened these together in such a way that it was virtually impossible for the cow to kick.

Hanging down from the ceiling behind each cow were two strands of binder twine. This was used to tie the cow's tail up. This way the cow couldn't use his tail to swat flies—or the milker. It is impossible to describe what it feels like to get belted across the side of the head by a cow's tail. It really hurts! How my brother Wayne would have appreciated these "conveniences."

After the milking was completely finished, Ted got to help the boys open the stanchions to release the cows from their stall. As soon as they had filed out, there were calves to be fed.

Another new experience for my grandson. All the boys helped feed the calves, including the five-year-old, Lynn. Lynn is the youngest and he's a charmer.

In the meantime, Becky had poured milk into a big pan to feed the impatient cats. Although they were "mewing up a storm," she never said a word about them talking to her. I guess maybe she doesn't let her imagination get away from her like Wayne did.

Andrew Yoder Sr., and his wife Clara, have owned the farm for some 45 years. Raised a big family there and now son Andrew Jr., and his wife Rose, have taken over.

All five of them make their parents proud.

Their son, Andrew Yoder 111, goes by the name of Maynard. Saves confusion. He's a lot of help to his dad even tho' he's only 12. Adam says he was named after the first man, Adam. Wa-a-a-ay after. But, he points out, the first Adam only had one name. This Adam has three names; Adam, Wayne, Yoder. Good point! Ruth was away when we got there. She had a job helping de-tassel hybrid corn. She still got home in time to help with the milking.

As we left the milking "parlor," the mama cat caught my eye. She "mewed" at me and I'm just sure I heard her say, "Keb-lar, it was nice having you here. Tum back some time, please!"

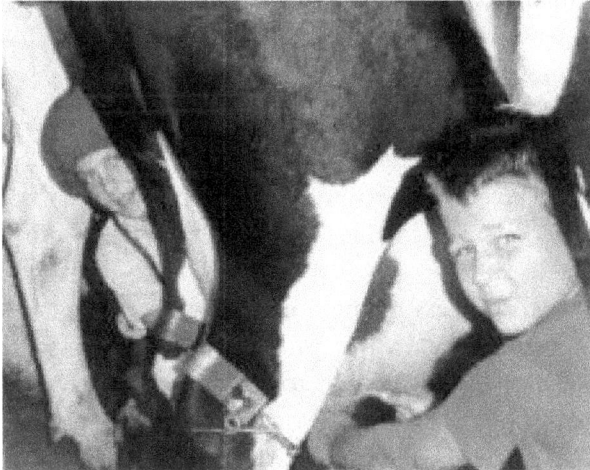

Adam Yoder and Ted Hewgley

27

Our Woods

*T*here wasn't another like it in the whole wide world—or at least I couldn't imagine one that could give as much pleasure as this one did. We lived on the farm where I was born until I was eight years old and then we had to move. Probably everything in the woods on that farm could have been found in some other woods, but not all in the same one. No! Never! Surely not! There were so many things in the woods to interest a little boy that I'm sure there's no way I can recall them all now. But let me try to bring some of them back to mind.

One of the things that gave us all a great deal of pleasure was mushrooms. By all, I mean my mom and dad and my five brothers and sisters. We always referred to gathering them as "hunting" mushrooms because they were usually camouflaged by blending in with the leaves or rotting stumps or whatever surrounded them where they happened to be growing. Not only was it a distinct pleasure to find them and to gather them, but it was an indescribable delight to eat them, for they were indeed a delectable delicacy.

We called them "sponge mushrooms" but I believe the proper name is "morel." They are the most delicious of all edible mushrooms. They look like cone-shaped sponges, pitted like a honeycomb. They are tan to brown in color with a short hollow, lighter-colored stem. As a matter of fact, the whole mushroom is hollow.

When we took them to the house after gathering them, Mom would cut them in half and put them in salt-water to soak overnight. That was guaranteed to kill any bugs that might have been in them. The next day, after rinsing them off, she rolled them in flour and fried them along with beef steak—if Dad could manage it—and we'd have a feast fit for a king.

My brother Wayne was by far the best hunter in the family, whether we were hunting mushrooms or cottontail rabbits. He was just about the greatest at a lot of things.

Growing boys never seem to get enough to eat and I guess maybe it was at least partly for that reason my three brothers, all older than I, were always on the lookout for anything they could eat.

We ate mayapples as they ripened. They grew on umbrella-shaped plants that we associated with mushrooms. We thought that if you found mayapples you were sure to find mushrooms. It weren't necessarily so. It would be the case more often if the mayapples were growing in heavy leaves or by a rotting log or even better, under a dead elm tree.

I can remember finding at least three different varieties of mulberries that ripened in the spring. Particularly, I remember one tree that had exceptionally long thin mulberries, lighter in color and sweeter than the regular blue ones. Never have seen any like it since.

Mom used to make mulberry pies. She liked to mix in a few sour cherries and it sure made a first-class pie. As I recall, the cherries and the mulberries ripened at about the same time in the spring.

I've got a story about my brother Charles and the big cherry tree that stood at the side of the front yard. But, that's a full-length story in itself.

Now then, it seems to me like it was my brother Lloyd that liked the Paw Paws that were so plentiful in late spring or early summer. They didn't taste that good to me, but I'd eat anything my brothers would eat and that didn't leave much out.

Black Haws were another of the wood's delicacies and there were lots of those. They looked like a small black button. They grew on low trees and had only one seed in them. Seems as though they were mostly skin, but we liked them.

There were berries of almost every kind—all wild. Like strawberries. No strawberry, whether it comes from California, Florida, Texas or anywhere else—tame—can hold a candle to wild strawberries. They have a unique flavor all their own. There were raspberries, blackberries, dewberries, and gooseberries. The wild gooseberries had stickers on the berries, but we hardly noticed them, and when they were ripe they made a scrumptious pie. My dad was especially fond of gooseberry pie.

And then there were little red apples no bigger than a small marble. They were kind of tedious to eat because of their size. They had four small seeds in them and the rest was all apple. Some city doctor would probably have said they weren't good for us, but we didn't know better. Hey! Maybe that's an example of "What you don't know won't hurt you."

There were pheasant and quail aplenty, but Dad never shot the quail and wouldn't let the boys shoot them either. However, pheasant, properly prepared, is gourmet fare. An epicurean delight.

Fox squirrels in the fall and cottontail rabbits in the winter were a staple of our farm diet. I even remember seeing flying squirrels gliding from an exceptionally big and tall elm tree. The first time I saw them "flying" it was almost beyond belief. There were several of them that took off at the same time. It seemed as though they just suddenly appeared in the air and were gliding along on the wind. Their legs were spread out as far as they could be and the skin between their legs was stretched taut so that they appeared to be nearly square. When they hit the ground some distance away, they seemed to land as smooth as a feather. Truly a wonder.

Raccoons. One night in late fall my brothers spotted some men cutting across our field some distance from the house heading toward the woods. Actually, the boys couldn't see the men. What they saw were their lanterns, and they could hear their dogs. The men were obviously going 'coon hunting. The boys couldn't see any reason to let just anybody hunt in our woods, so they called to them to find out who they were and just what they thought they were doing trespassing. The men ignored them and kept on going. After some discussion, my brother Wayne was sent to sneak back into the house and get the double barreled 12-gauge shotgun. This accomplished, Wayne called to the men to warn them that they had better turn back or suffer the consequences. They still were ignored, so Wayne "blasted away."

Now the men were so far away the shot couldn't have reached them, but in the still of the dark night they didn't know that. It sounded like a cannon. For sure it got their attention. It got Dad's attention, too. He came charging out the back door to see what in tarnation was going on. Turns out it was "Cobby" Van Wagner and some of his friends with their 'coon dogs. Cobby was by then frantically calling, "Cece! Cece! It's me, Cobby." Dad yelled to Cobby that it was all right, and after some confusion among themselves (and maybe taking another "bracer"), they started for the woods again. Lloyd and Charles and Wayne really "caught it."

Had we been aware when we were growing up, that 'coon meat was considered a delicacy by many people, we most certainly would have eaten them instead of just selling their pelts. That goes for 'possum, too, because there were plenty of them in the woods.

We also passed up another critter that I later found to be a culinary treat. Turtle. The ones that lived in the pond in our woods were about a foot across the shell. Looking back on it now, all I can say is that somehow we missed out on some good eatin'. There were lots of a smaller turtle that was only four or five inches across the shell. They usually hid under their shell when anybody or anything was around. Our dog "Shep" used to worry them—sniffing and pawing at them, trying to get them to stick their head out, without success.

Then there were bullfrogs. Now, they didn't get as big as Cuban bullfrogs—nowhere near—but, at night, they made enough noise to convince the uninitiated that they were veritable monsters.

I still remember the first time I had the "pleasure" of eating one. My brother Wayne caught several of them along the edge of the pond. Admittedly, the word "pond" is somewhat misleading in that all kinds of vegetation such as cattails, pussy willows and various reeds grew in it. Actually, the word "swamp" would be a more accurate description because it was really just a low area in "The Woods." Anyway, Wayne built a small fire alongside the pond to roast the frogs over. You would have to have been there in order to appreciate the way he killed and cleaned the frogs. He merely laid them across a stump and cut their heads off with a little old pocket knife Dad had given him. After that, it was a simple matter to skin and clean them. He then roasted the whole frog by putting it on a green forked stick that he had cut from a nearby limb. The stick had to be green or it would have caught fire. I can still see the flesh of the frog seem to crawl up the bones as it got hot and started to roast. Wayne said it was trying to jump even though it was dead. Wayne always liked everything burned—or at least crisp—so, actually, when it was done to his liking, the frog didn't look all that appetizing, but Wayne thought it was good. . . so, so did I.

Black walnuts! In the fall we had so many walnuts my brothers would put them in gunny sacks and haul them to the house on old Barney's back. He was our favorite horse—I've got a story about him, too. Husking and drying the walnuts was an art that I'll talk about another time. Hickory nuts. My memory says we had the biggest and best hickory nuts of anybody in LaGrange County.

And wait! You think pecans and English walnuts are good? You ain't tasted nothing yet, as the feller says, until you've tasted butternuts. Oh my! The chocolate fudge my sisters, Edie and Mary, used to make with butternut meats would have won ANY (pronounced eh-eh-eh-ne-e-e-e) candy-making contest, hands down. Their black walnut fudge would have won an easy second prize. I can feel a cavity coming on just thinking about how good it was. But you know, I haven't seen a butternut tree or even any butternuts since we left the farm. What a pity!

And then there were hazelnuts. They grew on bushes in the fence row. Not really in "The Woods" but close enough. The nuts grew in little clusters and when the weather turned to frost they would just sort of open up and there were the nuts. They weren't very big but we sure thought they were tasty. Haven't seen any of those bushes in years, either.

Something that was on many fences then but not now was bittersweet. It was a green vine that had green berries on it in the summer. There was sort of a shell on them and in the fall they would turn a beautiful orange color. This shell would kind of harden and then at the first frost they would open up, revealing the berry inside. This whole thing would dry and could be used for a bright-colored decoration in the house. It would last all winter before it would get really dry and start to sort of disintegrate.

My dad realized one summer that the low-lying area of "The Woods" was literally covered with spearmint. I don't remember that it grew there every year, but it was just about everywhere that year. Dad and my brothers spent at least a week mowing and drying what turned out to be a full hay wagon load of spearmint. Actually, they cut most of it with a scythe, because it wasn't that easy to maneuver the horse-drawn mower around the trees and other obstacles in the woods. After loading the dry mint on to the wagon, they set out for the mint still which was several miles away over on Highway. 20. Seemed like it took forever to steam or cook the mint, but when it was all over they had extracted five pounds of mint oil for which they paid Dad five dollars. I can still remember that the smell of mint was so strong my eyes watered. Looking back on it now I would judge that it would have cleared up any kind of sinus problem that anybody might have had.

One year nature supplied us with a special treat. A "Honey Tree." This big old tree was hollow and a big swarm of honey bees had taken up residence in it. All summer long they had built combs and filled them with honey from wild flowers and the big clover hay field right next to "The Woods." In the dead of winter, with snow on the ground and the bees dormant, Dad and the boys cut down the "Honey Tree." It was chock full of honey and I can still see Dad and his trusty knife cutting out the first honey-filled comb. There must have been ten gallons of honey altogether.

The main reason virtually every farm in Indiana had a "Woods" was that all the farm houses were heated with wood fuel. All cooking and baking was done with a wood-burning stove. These big old kitchen stoves always had a boiler at one end, used to heat rainwater for the ladies to use to wash their hair.

Dad and my brothers would cut down big trees with a cross-cut saw. Then Dad would cut most of the limbs off with his trusty double-bitted axe. The log would then be cut in firewood lengths with the cross-cut saw. The limbs that could be manhandled were piled so that when snow was on the ground they could be loaded on the bobsled and pulled up the lane to the back yard where they would be unloaded next to the buzz saw. That's a story all its own.

In addition to "The Woods" supplying our warmth in winter and some of our sustenance in summer and winter, it gave us many pleasures that I'll always cherish.

28

Uncle Floyd's Unusual Watchdogs

One of the joys of childhood is visiting relatives. And especially if there's somebody your own age to play with. No, not just to play with, but to *be* with. It's nice being part of a big family and having several brothers and sisters but, unless you're a twin, there's nobody your own age.

I especially remember a weekend I spent at Uncle Floyd Connelly's farm. Just me. None of my family was along. It was a most enjoyable time and I'm sorry only that it didn't happen more often. It's really peculiar how some memories will stick in your mind more than others. Almost like he was here now, I can see Uncle Floyd sitting in his rocking chair reading the newspaper and smoking his long-stemmed, small bowl pipe loaded with Prince Albert.

I remember wishing my Dad's "two-fer" cigars smelled so good. They called them "two-fers" because they cost two for a nickel. King Edwards, Golden Rods and Crooks are some I can remember.

Anyway, while Uncle Floyd read his paper, Aunt Eva would be talking to him and every so often he would go "Um-m-m-m!" sounding interested. Or "Ah-h-h-h-h" or "Oh-h-h-h" like he was just hanging on her every word. My cousin Arnold pointed that out to me or I might not have noticed.

Although Arnold and I didn't attend grade school together, we did attend and graduate from LaGrange High School together. I'm a little bit older than he is, but it's only a few months. We were good friends.

Aunt Eva was a good cook. Still is, for that matter. For supper we had a delicacy that I had never tasted before. Guinea hen. The biscuits and gravy, mashed potatoes, green beans and sweet corn I had had before, but Guinea hen? Never. It was delicious and Aunt

Eva was pleased at my high praise of the food. I ate until I was literally stuffed.

The next morning at breakfast I nearly negated her pleasure of the night before when I remarked at how small the fried eggs were. She said, rather testily, "You seemed to enjoy the guinea hen so much last night, I thought you'd like to try guinea eggs." I was very embarrassed and my face turned beet red. The guinea eggs might have been smaller, but they tasted every bit as good as chicken eggs.

Just before we went to bed, we listened to a radio program called "Little Jimmy" and the last thing he did at signing off was to sing a song that went this way:

"Now I lay me down to sleep,
I pray the Lord my soul to keep,
if I should die before I wake,
I pray the Lord my soul to take."

Later I found that this wasn't the only radio program they enjoyed. Just like Grandpa and Grandma Todd, it took a death in the family to keep them away from the radio show when Little Orphan Annie or Jack Armstrong, the All America Boy, was on. Two other favorites were "Amos and Andy" and "Fibber McGee and Molly."

Some people tend to put on a façade when company is present. This wasn't the case with Uncle Floyd and Aunt Eva. They were truly a peaceable, caring, loving couple.

Back to the guineas. Before Aunt Eva called Arnold and me into the house for supper, we had been walking around in the backyard. There was a thick grove of trees or maybe it was a woods alongside the yard. The guineas were getting ready to roost for the night in the tree branches. I asked Arnold why they didn't roost in the chicken house, since there was one. His answer was that guineas liked to be their own boss and didn't really like the idea of being domesticated. Guineas don't even get along with each other all that well and seem constantly to be bickering with one another. They have dark gray feathers with small white spots and, although they originated in Africa, they are a close relative of the ring-necked pheasant, which is impossible to domesticate.

After Arnold and I went to bed, we lay there talking, as boys will do. We heard a car coming and as it passed the grove of trees where the guineas were roosting, I heard the most gosh-awful racket I have ever heard in my life.

It was ever' last one of those guineas letting loose with continuous harsh cries—enough to frighten the bejabbers out of anyone. Arnold said they paid their board and room by acting as watchdogs. He said they'd carry on like that every time a car went by—or a man or dog or any other animal came near the house—and they did. For what seemed like all night long.

Uncle Floyd's guineas were indeed the most unusual watchdogs I've ever come across.

Aunt Eva and Uncle Floyd Connelly

29

The Mystery of the Little Grave

*T*he farm west of us was owned by "Uncle" Austin Merriman. His wife's brother, Dr. "Charlie" Miller, was married to my Aunt Mary, who was Dad's sister. So, we weren't really related except by marriage. No matter. We called him "Uncle" Austin.

There was a big mulberry tree in the fence row separating our farms. He never picked them, so we did.

Dad had several big tarpaulins that he used to cover wheat stacks. For one reason or another, Dad would stack wheat bundles maybe twelve to fifteen feet high and wait for the threshing rig to come around. He'd cover the wheat stacks with these tarps. Anyway, we'd spread one of these big tarps on the ground under the mulberry tree soon after the first one had ripened. We didn't dare wait too far into the season. If we did, the mulberries would commence getting little bitty bugs in them. They must not have been all that harmful because I'm sure we ate lots of them and it never hurt us.

After the tarp was spread, the race was on to see who could get up in the tree first. Then came all kinds of wild shaking and jumping up and down on the limbs. When all the berries were off that would come off, it was time to put them into buckets to take to the house. Mom would can some for use in the winter. But, she would also bake several delicious pies. Mom usually put some sour red cherries in the pie, too. M-m-m-m scrumptious!

Along this same fence was a long row of hazelnut bushes. We helped ourselves to these in the fall. Hazelnuts are actually small, wild, filberts.

Uncle Austin used the field across the fence as a cow pasture. The grass was grazed down fairly short, so it was easy for us to see the outline of the foundation where a house once stood. Many of the stones were still there. Also, there was an old pump, with the handle still attached, sticking up out of the ground. Maybe Dad told us who used to live there, but I don't remember that he did. There were six or eight gnarly old apple trees alongside what must have been the front yard. They still produced apples. Without worms, believe it or not.

However, the most mysterious item of conversation we ever found there was a small grave marker. It was in the fence row that separated the "yard" from the road in front.

Can you imagine the speculation? Maybe the child died right after it was born. Or perhaps it died from whooping cough. But we had all had it—and lived. How about German measles, or small pox? Could have been kicked fatally by a horse. That happens. Or Indians. They might have scalped it. We used to find arrow heads and even found an Indian grave.

We never found the answer but it made something interesting and mysterious to talk about. The one thing we agreed on was that it was the grave of a small child.

Somebody had lovingly set out lilac bushes by the grave. Or perhaps they had put the grave among the lilac bushes. Whichever, every spring the lilacs blossomed beautifully and fragrance of the purple blossoms were a subtle reminder of the "The Mystery of the Little Grave."

I had told my wife, Zena, about the grave. Her imaginative juices came up with another possibility. Her idea was—the family that lived there decided to move further west. There were rumors to be much better opportunities for good farm land, say, in Kansas.

True, this farm didn't look that productive. Some low places were unfit for crops. Lots of the surrounding area was covered with scrub bushes and dewberry vines. After many years of being farmed by Amish owners, it now looks like a virtual Paradise by comparison.

But, on with her vision. They had their furniture and farm tools all loaded on the covered wagon, even had the team hitched and their only milk cows tied behind.

Then tragedy struck. Little "Melissa," who had complained of not feeling well the day before, developed a very high fever and died. What to do? They buried her, wrapped in a comforter, among the lilac bushes.

And the headstone? The mother wanted the grave marked, so she had her husband remove the marble top from the small dressing table that had been one of the few things left from their former home in New England. Only when the headstone was placed did they start on their journey west.

Now, I ask you, how's that for imagination?

About twenty-five years after we had moved away, I returned. With my wife and daughters, Becky and Edie, we climbed the fence into what had been this front yard.

The old pump was gone. The apple trees were just a memory. Even the outline of the house's foundation was covered. And we couldn't find the grave marker. It could have been there, but the grass and weeds were a deep tangle and could have hidden it.

The lilac bushes had survived after all these years. And they were in bloom.

Remembering there was a stream of water in what would have been the very back yard, we had prepared a picnic basket to enjoy along its bank. Sure enough, we found a small meadow close to the stream and spread out our tablecloth.

The wieners hadn't been roasted, so we all set out to rustle up some firewood. Finally, we had enough to get a fire started. The wood was real dry and burned up fast. Zena thought it was kind of nice to see the rest of us cooking our own food and didn't want to interrupt us until we had eaten our fill. She volunteered to go hunt for more firewood

Now, I'll admit that I have heard some pretty loud yells in my lifetime and I'll also admit that I've long known that my wife had a tad of Cherokee blood coursing in her veins. But, I had never heard anything like the bloodcurdling scream that she let out when the stick she started to pick up rattled at her. It wasn't a stick. It was a rattlesnake.

"We've never gone back. And still, the "Mystery of the Little Grave" remains.

Tami
Brett

30

Butchering Day

"*I*n the good old days," many farmers butchered most of the meat consumed by their families. Included was beef, pork and chicken, at our house. I can't remember it happening with any regularity, especially beef. Fact of the matter, I only recall our butchering a beef one time. And then, it wasn't really a beef. More like a big calf. One thing for sure, it was really good.

Dad and my brothers butchered the calf. Mom and my sisters canned a lot of just plain chunks of beef. Canned it in two-quart fruit jars. I still remember the broth turning jelly-like when it cooled. During the winter it made some "mi-i-tee" tasty eatin' whether it was cooked with noodles or with dumplings. Mom made first class dumplings. Fluffy. I mean, always—fluffy.

The jelly off the beef was used to make gravy or just plain beef broth. Like soup. Maybe with potatoes and carrots or most any vegetables. Beef broth or chicken broth was what Mom fixed for us kids whenever we got sick. I can still hear her, "Eat this. It's good for you and it'll make you feel better." It did, too.

What Mom canned from the beef was mainly the front quarters. She'd cut all the meat off the bones and then the bones were used for soup. The ribs and the back, as well as the hind quarters, were hung in the combination garage-tool shed. It was cold winter and the meat stayed frozen—or near so—until it was eaten. And that doesn't take long, not with two adults and six kids that seem always to be hungry. At least once a week, we butchered a chicken, usually a rooster.

"Wait a minute!" I can hear you saying. "Butchered a chicken? Nobody butchers a chicken!" We did! What I mean is—we never raised any "fryers." You know—those little bitty two-pound chickens you buy at the supermarket? Mom never butchered a chicken until it weighed at least eight pounds—or thereabouts. That's as big as lots of people want their Thanksgiving turkey to be. Don't forget, Mom had to feed eight people each meal. You ever try to feed eight people with a two-pound fryer? No! Can't be done! Then again, Mom could make an eight-pound-plus chicken last for three meals.

Today, a generous serving of the main course would be eight ounces. So, it figures, an eight-pound chicken divided between eight people, some pretty small, would be a pound each. You see? Easily enough for two meals.

Mom could stretch it even further. For instance, she cooked the feet. Unless you've seen the feet on an eight or ten-pound Barred Plymouth Rock or a Buff Orpington chicken, you can't appreciate what I'm talking about. With gravies and soups, she stretched it to three meals.

Back to butchering. It may sound gross, as they say these days, but butchering a chicken was relatively simple. Obviously, first you had to catch the bird. Then you held it by the legs and put its head on a chopping block. Whack! With a hatchet, you chopped off its head! With your left hand, you gave it a heave and got it as far away from you as possible. If you didn't, you were covered with blood.

You've heard the expression, "Like a chicken with its head cut off." Well, they jump and thrash around until all blood and life are gone from them. It's like an instinct. As though the chicken knows all its blood is supposed to be drained out on the ground before its meat can be eaten.

There was always a big bucket of hot water waiting for the bird's last movement or death throes. Holding the chicken by its legs, it was dunked into the hot water. Then, holding the bird by the neck, ever so careful, the other side was lowered into the hot water. After this "scalding," the chicken plucking began. By dipping the whole bird in hot water, the feathers came out easily, and the skin came off the feet. Laugh! Go on, laugh! There's meat on the feet. I guarantee it.

Then, there's the matter of disemboweling the big chicken. Unless you've done it, you can't imagine the size of the heart, liver and gizzard of an eight or ten-pound chicken. These make up the giblets, which are all good eating.

Well, enough, already.

When the chicken is cut in pieces, ready to boil, it makes quite a mound of meat. Nothing like a fryer!

I'm not going to give any cooking lessons, but will move on to butchering a hog.

First, we needed a tripod. Dad had three poles that stood together with the proper arrangement of rope and pulleys.

Dad also had a 22 rifle. He felt that shooting it was the most effective and humane method of "dispatching" the "critter."

The boys coaxed the hog as close to the tripod as possible before Dad shot it, squarely in the forehead. Then a rope was attached to the hind legs so they could lift the hog up in the air. Next, its throat was cut so it would bleed freely.

I can't remember how they dunked the hog into the wooden barrel full of boiling water, but they did. That's what made it possible to scrape the hair off without too much trouble. Same theory as shaving, I guess.

While it was still on the tripod, it was a simple matter to slit the hog open and remove the "innards."

The tongue was saved as well as the heart and liver. The head was used to make "headcheese." Mom always pickled the feet. Nothing was wasted. Everything was used except the "oink" and the "squeal." Even the intestines were laid aside so they could be thoroughly cleaned and used for stuffing sausage.

It wasn't really a complicated process. The shoulders and the hams were saved for curing. Dad liked fresh "side meat" so, most of it was destined for early use.

The really interesting part of butchering a hog was, to me, rendering the lard, processing the "cracklings" and stuffing sausage. This was a day-long job, so it was done on the second day.

The fatty parts that couldn't be used for meat were cut into small chunks and were put into a big iron kettle over an open fire, and cooked. This is where the lard came from. Most farm women made soap from part of the lard, because there was generally more than they could use for cooking.

After the pieces of skin and fat reached a certain point of brownness, they were removed and put into the lard press. The same piece of machinery was used for stuffing sausage. The hot liquid lard was put in crocks or "lard cans."

Anyway, the chamber of the press was filled with pieces of this skin, fat and meat, and the cast iron cover put in place. By turning a crank, pressure was applied in order to squeeze out the last bit of lard. What was left was a cake—about two inches thick—of "cracklings." Another treat for kids "in the old days."

Everybody had a meat grinder. Mostly good meat and some fat pieces were ground together with proper seasoning to make sausage. Mom liked to season it mostly with black pepper and sage.

Some was kept to be eaten while it was fresh and still in bulk, but the casing sausage was "canned." She'd fry it until just brown, then put it in jars with some of the hot lard poured over it. Then the jars were turned upside down. The lard would go to the top of the jar and it helped seal it from the air. Pork chops were fried and put in one gallon crocks, then completely covered with hot lard.

The lard press was used to put the sausage into casings. The bulk sausage was put in the chamber, about two-gallon size, and the lid was then put on. By placing the cleaned hog intestines over the exit spout, then turning the crank to lower the compression lid, the sausage was forced into the casings—and—Voilà! Casing sausage.

Yes, indeed! Butchering day was one of the greatest experiences of growing up in "the good old days."

31

Flying Through Lightning Hollow

$\mathcal{D}$ad had some faults. Speeding was not one of them. Had he ever been stopped by a policeman—and I don't think he ever was—it would have been for obstructing traffic by driving too slow.

Now, procrastination was definitely one of his problems. He never said so, but I think his motto was, "Never do today what you can put off until tomorrow"—or even later.

"Preventive maintenance" was not in his vocabulary. Might not have ever heard the expression. I don't think he ever made any effort to fix his car—whatever was going wrong with it—until it would no longer budge. He originated the now common saying, "If it ain't broke, don't fix it."

Brakes? He never had a car that had any brakes. Well, he did have one. A brand new Model "T" Ford. It burned up in a fire at the farm before he had a chance to wear the brakes out. But, that's another story. The fire, that is. Yeah! I said, "before he had a chance to wear them out." He spent more time with his foot on the brake pedal than he did with his foot on the floor. I say on the floor because there wasn't any foot gas pedal. There were two levers that stuck out of the steering column just below the steering wheel. The one on the left was the spark and the one on the right side was the gas, or accelerator. You gauged your speed by adjusting the hand-operated accelerator.

Dad made real sure that he never drove over 25 miles an hour. He could just tell how fast he was going and if he felt that he was going faster he would ride his foot on the brake pedal. There were two other pedals on a Model "T", the clutch and the reverse. He spent enough time with his foot on the clutch that the clutch apparatus never worked right either. But don't fix it until it's completely worn out.

And gas. He was forever running out of gas. He almost never bought more than two gallons at a time.

I can still see him. Even though the gas pumps weren't self-service, he usually wanted to pump his own gas. There was a handle on the side of the pump. You had to work this handle from side to side to pump the gas out of the tank in the ground. After the big globe at the top of the pump was filled, you stopped and waited for it to kind of settle down.

It was fun to watch the gas coming into the globe. It came through the bottom and caused lots of bubbles while it was coming in.

Anyway, Dad would then put the gas nozzle in the automobile's gas tank. Most of his cars had the gas tank in front of the windshield and the gas cap was on top of it. Some of them had the tank under the seat. I don't think he ever had a car with the gas tank in the back.

Well, before he turned the pump on so it would let the gas run into the car, he'd always raise the hose up in the air, starting to drain the hose of gas. Then after he turned it on he'd watch until the gas came down to the two-gallon mark in the globe. As soon as it made a bubble he shut it off. He would then, again, almost ceremoniously drain the hose.

He always got his full two gallons. But he would still run out—which brings me to my story.

The family was headed toward town on a winter Saturday when we ran out of gas. We were a couple of miles west of town on the road that ran along the old Valley Line Railroad tracks. Out beyond the County Farm near Art Huff's farm.

I know it was just before Christmas because Dr. Shultz came gliding up in his big Buick and he had a big evergreen tree tied onto his back bumper.

He stopped alongside our car and hollered to Dad. "Can I help you?" Dad told him he sure could. Said we'd run out of gas and would he give us a push into town.

Doc says, "Let me get behind you so we can check to see if the bumpers meet," which he did and they did. Most car bumpers met in those days. Dad got back into our car and motioned Doc to come on and he did. Oh! How he did.

It wasn't any time at all until the telephone poles were going by so fast they looked like a picket fence. Dad had never driven—let alone just steered—a car that fast before.

We boys were having the thrill of our lives. We were laughing and shouting with joy and must have been standing up because Pa kept yelling for us to shut up and sit down. He was scared and real mad.

When we got to the Old Road 9 on the edge of LaGrange, Doc Shultz wanted to turn right, so he let up on the gas expecting us to slow up so we could turn right, too. The closest filling station was a place called the Old Log Cabin back to the right on US 20. But Dad didn't have any brakes and was going so fast he couldn't turn. We just shot over Road 9—I know the wheels left the ground—and on another block where we went flying down Lightning Hill through the Hollow, past the city dump, and back up the other side. I think the word "careening" might fit, too. We were still going fast enough to carry us all the way to Road 9. By then we had slowed down enough to be able to turn left and coast into Henry Burr's Texaco station.

That had to be the fastest, "funniest" ride we boys ever had, before and since—bar none.

Dad said some terrible things about Doc Shultz, including questioning his ancestry as well as his legitimacy.

The next week, Dad and Ray Combs fixed the brakes.

Pa would like to have, but none of us ever forgot the time we went "Flying through lightning Hollow."

32

"Yer in Hail! That's Whur Yar!"

I don't remember ever laughing at anybody's accent. I mean it! Now, I might have enjoyed somebody's accent enough to laugh, a time or two. But, to laugh at it, I never meant to.

It's well known, by Indiana natives, that "Hoosiers" have no accent. At least, I never thought so, until—When I first came to Houston, I took a position with the best truck line in the United States—bar none, Roadway Express.

Sales Representative. Never had the title of salesman before and some day I may tell the story about how I got the job. Andy Emerson was assigned the task of showing me the ropes. Andy told me I acted more like a farmer than a salesman. "You need a gimmick. Every successful salesman has a gimmick," Andy said. "Work on it. Come up with something."

On one of our first calls, I found my gimmick. When Andy introduced me to the customer, I shook hands with him and said, "Hello." Then when I was introduced to his secretary, who sat across the desk from her boss, I again shook hands and said, "Hello." Both of them seemed to be amused and with a smile in their eyes, they hung on my every word as I presented my "sales pitch."

All of a sudden the man turned to his secretary and in his excitement nearly shouted, "I know who he reminds me of! Herb Shriner."

"Yes! Yes! He not only sounds like him, but he looks like him," she answered.

The look in Andy's eyes said, "You've got your gimmick! Go for it." I turned and walked over to the door where we had entered the office. When I turned and started walking back, I had my left hand in my pocket and I was looking down at the floor. As I got to his desk, I ran the fingers of my right hand through my hair kind of like I was scratching my head. Then, I looked up at them and said, simply, "Hello."

They nearly cracked up laughing. But, they weren't laughing at me. They were just appreciating my Hoosier accent. They were laughing with me. You see, I had my gimmick all the time and didn't realize it. Shucks, I never did think I looked like Herb Shriner, though.

The reason I mention this experience is to clear a path to tell of something that happened to my brothers when we were kids on the farm. A family from Kentucky had moved onto a neighboring farm.

It was a rarity to get new neighbors. "Foreigners," Dad called them. Well, not really. But, we seldom saw anybody from a state other than Indiana. Then, when I heard Ray Combs talk, I was just sure he was from another country. Even though he was speaking English, I had trouble understanding him.

One day Dad had the left side of the hood up on his Model "T" just looking at it. Although he never claimed to be a mechanic, Dad could sometimes figure out what was wrong. The Model "T" engine was not all that complicated. Anyway, I was out in the yard when Ray walked up to the car and helped Dad stare at the motor. Then, Dad went into the garage to get some sort of a tool. By that time, Ray was really engrossed with something under the hood.

Ray abruptly raised up and turning toward the garage he called out in the accent that is typically unique to the Kentucky hills, "See-e-e-sul! Ye git me a par-r-r o'plahers, a haimer and some baylin war-r-r and ah kin fix this h'year 'T' Model."

My brothers and I had trouble holdin' back real genuine guffaws. To that point in our lives, it was one of the funniest sounds we had heard. We never really got used to it, ever.

Another time, in early winter, Charles and Wayne were hunting cottontail rabbits with Ray. The boys were spread out in a field of wheat stubble, walking along with Ray somewhat in the lead. Ray suddenly stopped, and turning his head toward Charles and Wayne, he shouted, "Be quite, boys! Be quite! Ah sees a ray-but." By the time the boys got through laughing, the "ray-but" was long gone.

Before I tell the next one I need to make mention of something that plays an important part in the story. The ministers at Bethel Church had instilled a great fear in us boys. A fear of "hell fire and brimstone" and of the devil. Hardly a Sunday went by that we weren't told that good people went to heaven and bad ones went to hell. Now I've said it. On with the story.

I've reported before that all three of my brothers were climbers. On this occasion, Ray Combs was with them back in the big woods. I don't really know what they were doing, but there was plenty to do. Even just plain walking. Nothing could be much more relaxing and enjoyable than a walk in the woods.

They watched a big red fox squirrel scampering along on the ground. He took a big jump and landed about six feet up the trunk of a giant oak tree. No more did he touch the tree than he darted around to the blind side.

The boys ran around the other side and the squirrel changed sides, still going up. Then he scrambled into his nest which was out on a limb between 40 and 50 feet from the ground. This was too much of a temptation. Up the tree they went with Lloyd in the lead. Ray stayed on the ground.

I don't really believe they had any particular plan of action. Pretty sure not.

When Lloyd reached the limb the nest was on, he started inching out on it toward the nest. He was holding on with both hand, had his legs around the limb and even his feet were holding on.

Just as he was able to reach out and touch the nest, it happened! The squirrel came zooming out of the nest and with all claws extended, he tore along Lloyd's hands, arms, head, body and legs. Lloyd promptly let go with his feet and legs—still holding on with his hands. But—the weight of his whole body suddenly coming to bear on the very end of the limb, it broke, and down he came.

Another limb, about 10 feet further down, broke some of the fall and stunned him. When he hit the ground, he landed face first on a big root of the tree. Unconscious! Completely out cold!

Charles and Wayne were really scared because Lloyd was laying so still. They started climbing down out of the tree so fast it's a wonder they didn't fall.

Ray started nudging Lloyd with his foot. "Git up, Loyud! Git up! Ye ain't hurt none. Git up! They ain't nuthin' wrong with ye! Git up!"

The boys finally got to the ground and stopped Ray from kicking at Lloyd and yelling at him.

They all pulled Lloyd over to the tree and propped him up against it. His face was bloody and his nose was literally crushed. Finally, he started to come around. "What happened?" he mumbled.

Not one to miss an opportunity for a good joke, Ray answered, "Ye done fail outen a tree an kilt yerself! That's whut haypened."

"But . . . but . . . where am I?" Lloyd stammered.

Louder than before, Ray answered, "Yer in Hail! That's whur y'ar! Yer in Hail."

With eyes wide open now, Lloyd asked, "Well—then—who are you?"

Building to a real red-faced crescendo, Ray shouted, "Ahm thuh Day-vil! Who'd ye 'spect to find in Hail?"

Whereupon, Lloyd fainted dead away.

33

The Pickle Patch

$\mathcal{D}$ad raised an acre or more of "pickles" every year. I grew up calling cucumbers, "pickles." Maybe it was because Dad always took them to the "Pickle Factory."

Or maybe it had something to do with the tongue twisters Uncle James Woodworth taught us. Uncle James was an auctioneer and they taught him lots of tongue twisters at Auctioneering School.

> As I recall, a particular one went:
> Peter Piper picked a peck of pickled peppers,
> A peck of pickled peppers Peter Piper picked.
> If Peter Piper picked a peck of pickled peppers,
> Where's the peck of pickled peppers Peter Piper picked?

Uncle James would encourage us to say it as fast as we could. Try it!

One of the fields at the back of our farm was on kind of a hill. The fence that separated us from the neighboring farm came across the ridge. The side of this ridge was sort of a mixture of sand and gravel and this seemed to be just what "pickle" plants thrived on.

One of the reasons Dad liked the idea of this particular crop was that it was ready for market at a time when none of the other crops were. Early in the spring was the time to ready the field for planting. Then plant as soon as possible. They could even stand a mild frost. I remember when it was picking time the weather could get downright brisk.

About the only cultivating that was done was with a hoe. Only rarely could you get through the patch even once with the corn cultivator. Once the plants came up, it didn't take long before they started vining in every which direction. That's why the cultivator wasn't of much use.

The cucumbers were picked every day, except Sunday, and the earlier in the morning the better. If they're not picked early in the morning they won't be crisp and the factory won't take them. All the boys helped Dad with the picking. I don't remember my sisters helping. Maybe they did. There was never any doubt in our young minds that this back-breaking labor was designed as some kind of punishment for farm boys.

Dad used to promise to pay us so much for each bucket of cucumbers we picked. I don't remember that he ever wound up paying us anything.

After we'd pick a bucket full, Dad would pour them into a burlap bag. We used to have as many as ten bags full.

After the pickles were taken to the house, Dad would spread them out on a big tarpaulin and sort them. Ounce for ounce, the real small ones brought a much higher price than the next larger size, and so on. The pickle factory wouldn't take the really big ones, so those were turned back to Mom. She put them up in big 5-gallon crocks so we could have dill pickles in the winter time. She made mouth watering de-e-e-licious sweet pickles and bread and butter pickles from the big ones, too. Mom was a good all-around cook. Nothing ever very fancy. Just plain old country cookin'.

Back to sorting pickles. "Grading them," as Dad would say. They were supposed to be sorted, or graded, before being taken to the pickle factory. The reason for that, later. The different sizes were put into their individual burlap bags and loaded into the back seat of the Model "T" Ford. Sometimes, when there were too many, some of them were put between the fenders and the hood.

Before I was old enough to go to school, I used to get to go along to deliver the pickles to the factory. Even after starting school I got to go and so did one or more of my brothers. It was a special treat.

The factory was located on the west side of the Pennsylvania Railroad tracks south of US 20. We never seemed to get there first, so we had to get in line. Sometimes there would be ten or more cars, trucks or buggies ahead of us. When the line seemed to be moving too slowly to suit him, Dad would get impatient and go inside to see what the hold up was. Likely as not, the slowdown would be caused by somebody who had a big pickle patch and a lot of sacks of "unsorted" pickles. That would upset Dad no end. It would likewise upset Vern Beaty who ran the pickle factory. It made his job much more difficult.

I can't at his late date remember if Mr. Beaty sat at the end of this long sorting table or at the side, but his size and demeanor made him seem like a "Grand Patriarch." He just plain commanded respect.

One thing I noticed was that when Dad was immediately behind a farmer who had not pre-sorted his pickles, Mr. Beaty would make a point of holding up the man's check so he'd have to stand around for a while and could see how easy it was to process Dad's pickles. Then he'd praise Dad.

We always liked that. Dad didn't get much praise from anybody.

There was another thing about the pickle factory that was a mystery to me. I used to watch this old man, at least I thought he was old, push a wheelbarrow into a room that was filled with salt. I just couldn't imagine so much salt. Loose. This man wore knee-length rubber boots. He'd walk right in and shovel salt into the wheelbarrow. He'd then wheel the loaded wheelbarrow over to these absolutely huge vats that were being filled with pickles. Using his shovel, he'd throw the salt into the pickles and go back for another load.

Another mystery was, after all this careful sorting of cucumbers they unceremoniously dumped them, all sizes, into the same vat. Mixed together. Just like they came from the patch. Enough to make a kid question the intelligence of adults.

Raphael, one of Mr. Beaty's several sons, explained it to me one day. Simply, there was another sorting. At another "Pickle Factory." The cannery.

History has a way of repeating itself.

For about twelve years, my wife and I owned a small farm on the north side of Lima High School in Howe.

One year—just one year—I raised an acre of cucumbers. Bill Fegley ran the "Pickle Factory" then and he talked me into it. Said it would be good for my daughters, Becky and Edie. Fact is, they considered it cruel and inhuman punishment. They never forgave me.

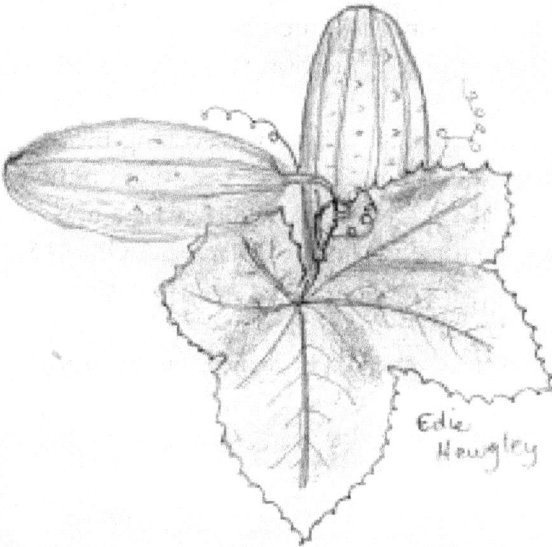

Edie Hewgley

34

Green School

*W*hen I was young, my Dad used to say, "You'll never learn anything if you don't ask questions." True. On the other hand, when we asked him a question more than likely he'd say, "Go ask your Mother."

Maybe, just maybe, that's why it was so long before I found the answer to a question that came into my mind on the first day of school. "Why is this big red brick school, with a gray slate roof and windows and trim painted white, called the 'Green' School?" I wondered.

It wasn't all that big, I don't guess, but it seemed big to me. Bigger than our house even though it only had one room besides the cloak room.

I have some memories about that cloak room I'd just as soon forget.

As I recall, the first year I was in school there were 45 students divided between eight grades. The class enrollment varied from three to ten pupils with each class taking from four to six subjects.

Poor teacher! What a challenge. In addition to handling all these classes, she was school-ground monitor, baseball umpire, arbitrator of every kind of dispute—and on top of that—she was expected to handle janitorial duties. This included keeping the school room clean and stoking the furnace—unless she could get the students to do it for her.

The first year I attended Green School, my teacher was Miss Ruth Ireland. She only taught there one year, as I recall. Seems as though she had a problem disciplining the older boys.

Miss Ireland was replaced by Amos 0. Hostetler. Nobody that I know of can recall his having any ongoing problem with discipline. Mr. Hostetler meted out punishment swiftly and with no bias. He had no favorites or "pets."

Back to the subject of the red brick school called Green. In the mid 1800's, my great grandfather, Jim Green, owned the farm across the road, called the Black Walnut Farm. He also owned the farm on the east side known in later years as the Dan Doney Farm. He had only two children, both girls. They were given names we would now consider unusual, to say the least. One was named "Icey" and the other "Mate." That would have made them Icey Green and Mate Green.

Great Grandfather Green must have owned more than those two farms—perhaps the one later known as the Ora Anderson Farm. It was on this farm that the Green School House was built. Grandpa Green donated the land and then helped build it. So, it figures that the school would rightly be called Green School.

At the time of its construction, it was the only school for miles around. Dad used to tell about the boys riding horses to school. The pupils walked most of the time.

Of course, Grandma and her sister, Mate, attended Green School. Dad and his four brothers and two sisters all went the full eight years. And my two sisters and three brothers attended there, too. Some of the other names Dad mentioned were Miller, Campbell, Bontrager, Shupp, Lattie, Doney and others.

I particularly remember him talking and laughing about a fellow student named Andrew Gable. When the teacher had his back turned, like when he was writing a lesson on the blackboard, and there was any kind of loud or uncalled for noise, the teacher would assume that Andrew was the instigator. He'd wheel around and, pointing his finger, he'd say, "An-n-n-dr-ew-ew-ew-ew, was that yew-ew-ew?" That would bring on spontaneous laughter from everybody and cause Andrew to be sent outside—guilty or not.

My memory says the Green School house had a belfry. That's another "thing of the past." It was amazing how much faster I could run when I heard the bell ring. Now, it's all done electronically.

Even though teachers had charge of the children some eight hours a day, they were shamefully underpaid, almost without exception. It was for this reason, during Dad's time and before, the teacher would take turns staying in different parents' homes. So, in effect, their salary included board and room.

Teachers were expected to be a good example in many ways. Conduct? Had to be exemplary. Clothing? Were supposed to look almost as good as their Sunday best.

The school house was also used as the community gathering place. Different types of business meetings were held there as well as the celebration of certain holidays.

One of the most fun meetings I can recall was when everybody—the whole family, I mean—would bring food and we would have a "pot luck" supper. After we had eaten and everything was cleaned up and put away, we'd have a spelling "bee."

Everybody, parents and all, would stand around the outside of the room. We'd have a spell down. If you missed a word, you were eliminated. You got only one chance. The teacher was always in charge and he or she would use the school spelling book. If you were in the first grade, you got a first grade word. Second, you got a second grade word, and so on. The words for the parents would be taken from the eighth grade part of the speller.

The excitement was high as the children tried hard to be still standing after their parents had missed a word and had to sit down. It sure made spelling a lot more interesting and encouraged all the children to study harder.

Now, the Green School House is gone, but not the memories. The land has reverted back to the farm from whence it was separated. Ah, well. How dear to my heart are the memories of my childhood.

Green School
LaGrange County   Clay Township
1930-31
Teacher

Amos O. Hostetler
Arthur G. Huff, Trustee   Fred M. Hostetler, Bus Driver

Pupils

Grade 8: Margaret Bradley, Winford Lewis

Grade 7: Mae Schrock, Rosalie Anspaugh, Margaret Doney, Marion Atwater

Grade 6: Ruth Mishler, Bonniegean Hope, Milbourn Norris, Roy Foltz, Evelyn Stewart, Mary Lucile Seaney, Charles Woodworth, Ernest Gooch

Grade 5: Byron Foltz, Wayne Lewis, Thomas Bradley, Wayne Woodworth, Angeline Partheen

Grade 4: Nedra Norris, John Robert Doney, Esther Hooley, Charles Stewart, Paul Anspaugh

Grade 3: Lois Mishler, Robert Noel, Clarence Seaney, Elmer Neff, Naomi Hooley, Ted Woodworth, Paul Bradley, Donovan Eagleson

Grade 2: Junior Hostetler, Clarence Lewis, Vernon Neff

Grade 1: Donabelle Eagleson, Esther Neff, Marion Jean Seaney, Rachel Sweet, Ernest Neff, Paul Neff.

35

Charles Lindbergh and the Spirit of St. Louis

*O*lder people know how early impressions last longer than any others. Indelibly implanted in my memory bank is a picture of Charles Lindbergh and his Spirit of St. Louis. I'm not an artist, but I could come close to drawing a reasonable facsimile of this "early impression." There it was, hanging next to Abraham Lincoln. I don't remember George Washington being there, maybe he was, but Lindbergh and Lincoln were definitely there. Somehow, I don't recall any other pictures on the wall in the school room at Green School.

Actually, both Lindbergh and Lincoln made a great impression on me as time moved along. But, at the first moment of my seeing him there, a thrill of excitement that is impossible to describe passed through me.

A boy's imagination can do some amazing things, and this little farmer boy's imagination really soared. Many's the time I daydreamed of the "Lone Eagle" and me flying together.

I fantasized flying with him to California, which I had heard was the most beautiful place in the world. We flew over big groves of orange and grapefruit trees, and immense forests of redwood trees. Grandpa Todd had once sent us a postcard showing a redwood tree so huge that a road had been made through it. The card had an automobile right in the tree.

And, of course, we flew from New York City to Paris. Its reputation as "Gay Paree" made it sound like an exciting place to see. It was 1927 when Lindbergh flew solo, nonstop, across the Atlantic from New York to Paris. It was a feat of daring that captured the entire world's heart.

Watching a Public Broadcasting System program titled "The American Experience" reminded me of Charles Lindbergh, again.

This show was billed as a triumphant true-life adventure story, "The Great Air Race of 1924." It seems the producers had located an abundance of movie footage of this first flight around the world. The newsreels had sent cameramen to cover it. And they really did; they went to Japan, to India, and to Greenland.

In 1924, airplanes were called "flying coffins." They were made of wood and canvas. They had open cockpits and one engine. Airfields and weather stations were virtually unheard of.

As the documentary unfolded, eight Americans (four Army pilots and four mechanics) were determined to fly their airplanes around the world. Four of them made it. They flew something over 26,000 miles. It took them 176 days to circle the globe, and they touched down in 29 countries along the way. When they landed safely home in Santa Monica, California, a crowd of 200,000 was at the airport to greet them, and one full acre of the landing field was strewn with roses. Quite a reception! Their fame was short-lived, although their incredible feat of courage and endurance has never been duplicated.

When Charles Lindbergh flew across the Atlantic three years later, he won the glamour and the glory. I guess that included having his picture hang alongside Lincoln at Green School.

As a general rule, teenagers can't tell you what they want to be when they grow up. However, from age six to twelve, they always know exactly what they're going to be. There was no doubt in my mind what I wanted to be. An aviator.

Like the story of the Great Stone Face, I watched the picture of Lindbergh so much that my brothers said I was beginning to look just like him. That was music to my ears, although they probably weren't serious. I always thought he looked more like my brother Wayne.

Zena said when a plane flew over the little one-room school she attended in Kansas, the teacher would take the kids out to watch. My wife likes to tell everybody she started school when she was four years old. It's true. But, two days later she was five. Her first grade teacher's name was Verdeen Fields and she was sixteen. Both just kids, Zena says.

Her second grade teacher was Gertie Van Dreet. She was enough older that she reminisced, "When I was in school, the teacher used to let us go out to watch the few automobiles that passed by."

Two of Zena's sisters, Mildred and Opel, taught grade school after they graduated from Lebanon High School. The pay was $30 a month.

Well, I didn't become a pilot. But flying never lost its fascination. Every chance I got I would fly. Still do.

The first plane I flew in was an open cockpit two-seater. One seat behind the other. The pilot was Beaty Hostetler. An excellent pilot, and I trusted him. Maybe that's why I've never had any fear of flying. He and my brother Lloyd have always been good friends.

Beaty used to wear black boots and the pants that pilots wore then. They looked like riding breeches. Ray Fisher, who was a state policeman, wore the same outfit. Another thing they shared with Charles Lindbergh was the leather cap with the chin strap and goggles. Those leather caps caught on in a hurry and every boy wanted one just like the Lone Eagle wore.

While a guest of Uncle Sam in the 1940's, I visited the National Air Museum of the Smithsonian Institution in Washington, D.C. There I actually got to see the Spirit of St. Louis. The same excitement I had felt in 1928 took hold of me again. I felt like I was looking at history and I was. But it had been less than 20 years. History will never stop being made until the end of this system of things.

What do you suppose ever happened to that picture? I'd sure like to have it.

36

"Teddy Bear, Get in Here!"

$\mathcal{M}$y daughters, Becky and Edie, were pleading with me to drive them to school. Though our small farm adjoined the Lima High School playground on the north, it was about four blocks to the front entrance of the school on the south.

In spite of the fact it was called Lima High School, all twelve grades attended and in the same building.

Across the road to the west was the Howe Military School.

The incident I was talking about occurred around the winter of 1952. That means Becky was ten and Edie six. Or somewhere near that. On the morning in question, the temperature had dropped to below zero and there was six or eight inches of snow on the ground.

Now, I had every intention of driving them to school and in fact, did. But, it seemed a fair chance for some good-natured ribbing. They now claim that I told them, "When I was your age, I walked five miles to school. Often in temperature well below zero and with snow drifts up to my armpits. And up hill all the way—in both directions."

Well-1-1-1 now-w-w-w, I don't think I'd have stretched it that much. Not five miles. It was a little over one, but not five. And it wasn't up hill in either direction. But, the rest of it's true.

We sure didn't get to stay home just because we had a foot or even more of snow and the temperature was below zero. We just thought it was a fact of life.

The first year I went to school, all three of my older brothers attended Green School with me. Lloyd was in the eighth grade and he would break trail when there was heavy snow on the ground. Either Charles or Wayne followed him and I brought up the rear.

Now, I've said many times that every dark cloud has a silver lining. Weather like this and having to trudge through it had to be considered a dark cloud. Sometimes it takes a lot of imagination to find it and sometimes you have to sort of make your own silver lining. This was one of those times.

Even though my brothers were "breaking trail" for me, I still fell down with some regularity, especially when the snow was really deep. I promise you, it gets deep, on occasion, in Northern Indiana. Anyway, I was covered with snow and half frozen by the time I got to the Foltz farmhouse.

Many's the time my brothers would go on ahead and leave me behind. When they did that, I'd tromp up onto the Foltz porch and knock on the door thinking that maybe I'd ask what time it was.

Hattie Foltz would come to the door wiping her hands on her apron. The minute she opened the door, she'd grab me by the arm and shout, "Teddy Bear, get in the house! Land sakes! You look to be frozen stiff. Let me help get your mittens and coat off. Stand over here by the stove and warm yourself while I fix you some hot chocolate and I'll see if I can't find some sugar cookies."

"Rube" Foltz would sweep the snow off me as I stood by the fire. Their boys had already left for school, most likely having joined my brothers. In no time at all I was warmed through and through. Their old pot bellied stove and big kitchen range put out a tremendous amount of heat. Having drunk the cocoa and eaten the sugar cookie, Hattie'd put my coat and mittens back on me and with an admonition to "hurry on to school now" she'd give me another sugar cookie and "shoo" me out the door.

See? I made my own silver lining. My Dad didn't raise no dumb kids!

Back in 1977, 1 decided to take early retirement. That's when I discovered that I hadn't been born.

In order to retire and draw a pension from Roadway Express, I had to produce a birth certificate. So, I sent off to the right people at Indianapolis for this document. They're the ones who told me that I didn't exist. At least, not on paper. They had no record. No certificate.

"All right. Let's go back to the beginning. Let's try the LaGrange Court House," I'm thinking to myself. Again, no record. No certificate. All my brothers and sisters were listed there. Not me. They did tell me what documents I could use to get a "Delayed Registration of Birth."

1. An infant baptismal certificate. Didn't have one of those. I was baptized at the Mt. Zion Evangelical Lutheran Church when I was seventeen. That's not exactly infant. Unacceptable.

2. School records for the first grade. Didn't have those either. Seems like the school records for Green School were kept at County Commissioner Ivo Christler's house. Unfortunately, the house burned down. The records were destroyed. I did get a letter from Don Presdorf attesting to the accuracy of this information. He now lives on Ivo's farm. They accepted that. Got another letter from Amos Hostetler verifying that I had attended Green School. They took that, also.

3. Birth certificates for my children. I can't imagine how that proved anything other than Becky and Edie's birth, but they accepted those.

4. Military Records. I had those.

5. Records from an old family Bible. I didn't have that either, but I came up with something a lot more interesting and the people of Indianapolis thought so, too.

My wife Zena, my daughter Becky and her two daughters, Edie and Sharon, were with me as I drove into the yard of the Old Gushwa Farm. This farm now belongs to Byron Foltz. His mother, Hattie, lived with Byron and his wife Margaret. I can't remember exactly what month it was, but I do remember that it was green bean picking time. Not cold weather. Definitely, not cold. When I knocked on the door, I heard someone inside, "Just a minute." Then, through the screen door, I saw this little white haired lady coming toward me wiping her hands on her apron. She'd been snapping beans. When she got to the door, she looked up at me and said, "Yes? May I help you?"

"Do you know where a fellow could get a cup of hot chocolate and a sugar cookie?"

With the most surprised and pleased look on her face that I've ever seen, she threw the door open and grabbing me by the arm, she shouted, "Get in here, Teddy Bear, before you freeze to death!" We hugged each other and cried tears of joy. It had been a long time. Too long. But, she remembered.

We called for my family to join us and we sat around the dining room table talking and getting acquainted. Margaret was a gracious host. She served us iced tea and—you guessed it—sugar cookies.

Finally, I asked Mrs. Foltz if she could remember when I was born. Her memory was unbelievable. She said, "Of course I can. You were born on Aug. 4, 1922. Your brother Wayne was born on Aug. 2, 1919." She remembered all of us.

"How in the world can you remember when we were born?"

"I took care of your brothers and sisters when you were born. Land sakes! You were a big one. Your brother, Wayne, weighed 11½ pounds. But, you weighed 12½ pounds. I've never seen such big babies."

"But, I have a good way to refresh my memory. Let me show you." Walking over to a beautiful old glass-fronted cabinet, she drew out a book to show me. It was a birthday diary. She pointed out to me the listing of the birth dates of me and my siblings as well as all our children. She had been, in effect, following us all these years. There were many, many more birth dates listed, but I was mainly interested in my own.

The photostat of that one page was the clincher. The Indiana State Board of Health sent me a "Delayed Registration of Birth." It's a great relief to know that I was born, after all.

37

Wayne and His Stilts

*M*y brother Wayne was known as "Slim" by most of his friends. But, not by his family. We called him Wayne. That's the way our folks wanted it. No nicknames. Any of us.

Nicknames aren't always accurate. Now you take my brother Wayne. When he went into the army during World War II, he was six foot three inches tall and weighed 145 pounds. Now, that's slim, so the name fit him to a "T". However, by the time he was about 35 he weighed 250 pounds. That's not exactly slim, but then again, he wasn't fat by any stretch of the imagination. Still, his friends continued to call his "Slim."

With a little bit of effort at promotion, he could as well have been known as "Stilts" all his life. Let me tell you about it.

When I was little we had a reasonably new barn on our farm. It seemed like a big one to me. One thing I remember for sure. It had way more stalls than we had horses. We just had Barney and Prince. Those extra horse stalls figure in my story.

Now, there's no way to tell where Wayne came up with this bright idea. On the other hand, it might have been Lloyd or Charles that conjured it up. Wayne decided to make some stilts.

I hadn't thought about this in years, but a while back, when Zena and I were vacationing with Ed and Elaine Brown, we saw a clown on stilts. He was wearing the whole clown costume and long pants clear to the ground. As we watched him, it reminded me of my brother Wayne. Not the clown. The stilts.

Anyway, the partitions between the horse stalls were solid wood at the bottom. But, up about five feet and on to the ceiling, the dividers were one inch by two inch boards. Since they weren't planed, they were a full one inch by two inches thick and made of wood that was heavy and hard. Elm, or something like that.

After a lot of prying, the boys managed to get two of the longest boards off. They were at least twelve feet long. Next, they had to build a foot platform. A step, in other words. This needed to be about three to four inches wide or as wide as Wayne's foot. One step for each stilt. This was done by cutting three pieces of one-inch wood two inches wide and about six inches long, then nailing them to the long piece, one on top of the other.

Wayne was only ten or eleven at the time, so the top of the stilts would need to be about to his shoulders. For this reason, the step was put about four feet from the top, thus making the step eight feet from the ground.

In order to help hold his feet on the step and in order to help lift the stilts, they next nailed a strip of harness leather over the step. It was kind of like having your foot in a stirrup.

Getting onto the stilts was another matter that took some doing. He finally solved the problem by leaning the stilts against a limb of the russet pear tree and then climbing the tree. From this vantage point, he stepped onto the stilts. Voilà! An eight-foot extension to his legs.

That had to be a classic example of starting at the top. Probably it would have been easier to start with two-foot stilts, but no. He started with eight-foot ones. Without having had any previous experience, Wayne took to stilt-walking like a duck takes to water. Good balance is essential. He had it.

Off to school we went. The rest of us were running to try to keep up with Wayne. Byron Foltz was just leaving his house on his way to school. When he saw us coming, he hurried back into the house and soon the whole family was out in the yard to watch "Stilts" and his six-foot stride. Byron and Roy and Granville Foltz joined the parade to school. Just before reaching Green School, our destination, the Doney family came out to see what was going on. Then, John and Margaret joined us. Wayne was having so much fun leading this parade, that he overshot the school yard and went on down to the corner where the Ora Anderson family lived. They came out to watch and Orene joined us on the way back to the school house.

Wayne was really in his glory as the parade followed him onto the school grounds to be joined by the other students. He was surrounded by admirers. But, all good things have to end.

Getting off the stilts was going to be a problem, but not for long. As Wayne backed up against the school house, he slipped his feet out of the stirrups and hand over hand climbed down one of the stilts.

Afterward, Wayne said he felt like he had been "king for a day."

38

My Defender, Brother Lloyd

*A*gainst his will, my brother Lloyd repeated the eighth grade. Dad said it wouldn't hurt him any. Seems as how Dad had taken the eighth grade several times. During my father's "day," it was the usual thing for farm boys to miss a lot of school. Likewise, it wasn't an easy matter for them to go to high school. Farming came first.

Since he wasn't going to attend high school, Dad kept going back to the eighth grade, off and on, until he was 21. It was legal even though he was graduated the first time around. And, it was free.

That wasn't the reason Lloyd repeated. He was expelled. And, just three days before school was out. Lloyd was never known for good timing.

On this occasion, all the kids were coming in from noon recess. They'd been playing baseball, which was the school's favorite sport.

Lloyd was just taking his seat when Roger Frisby threw his baseball glove at him. Hit him, too. The teacher was busy writing an assignment on the blackboard, so she didn't see what Roger had done. Lloyd picked the glove up off the floor and threw it back at Roger. Hit him, too. Teacher did see that. Expelled!

Like I said, Lloyd never did have good timing. Had this happened earlier in the school year, he'd have had time to fulfill a probationary period and then graduate. But, NO! Three days before school was out. Had to take the whole year over again.

The teacher was Daisy Mosier. When Lloyd got home and told Dad what had happened, he didn't anticipate the reaction he got from Dad. Seems as how Daisy Mosier had been his teacher, too.

Dad's comment was, "That old heifer never did like me and she's just taking her spite out on you."

Lloyd didn't go back until the fall classes started. I've never told him, but I was kind of glad it happened. That way, I was in the first grade and Lloyd was in the eighth. He was my defender.

Daisy Mosier didn't come back to teach at Green School. She was replaced by a pretty young lady whose name was Ruth Ireland. Miss Ireland only lasted one year—as I recall. Dad said she wasn't tough enough. He never thought any woman was "man" enough to handle some of the eighth graders, especially those who kept coming back until they were 21.

Her automobile was a black Model "A" Ford. (I mention that because it figures in my story.) Henry Ford would sell you a car painted any color you wanted—long as you chose black.

So—all Model "T" Fords and most Model "A" Fords were black. Later, the predominant color of the "V8" was black. Lloyd was not my only defender. My other brothers, Charles and Wayne, did their fair share of defending me. In this particular instance, they were all three involved. But, mainly Lloyd. His part I remember the most vividly.

There was a ditch along the road on two sides of Green School. When it rained to amount to anything, one could plan on there being about a foot of water standing in this ditch.

On this particular day it had rained most of the afternoon, but had stopped just before Miss Ireland dismissed school for the day. The ditch was chock full of water.

Now, according to my memory, Linton Norris threw my cap into the ditch. That's when the battle began. Lloyd against Linton—Charles against Harold Fryhover—and, Wayne against Milburn Norris. Maybe more, but that's all I can remember. And me? I just watched.

There was lots of pushing and hitting and wrestling. Before it was over, everybody had been in the ditch and was soaking wet—except me.

Dad had been a top notch country wrestler and boxer in his younger years, so he had taught Lloyd how to defend himself quite effectively. Finally, everybody stopped fighting with the exception of Lloyd and Linton. The others just watched, because those two were putting on quite an exhibition. They were about the same age and pretty evenly matched.

Evidently, Miss Ireland had been watching. She hadn't intended to intervene, until the boys bloodied each others' noses and started splattering blood on her black car. Even then, she didn't try to stop them. Miss Ireland locked the front door of the school and hurried to her car. They moved their fight away from it and she drove away.

By some sort of mutual agreement, they stopped fighting. Both the worse for wear and tear. To the best of my knowledge, they never fought each other again.

I thanked God for big brothers.

39

The Goodyear Blimp

*O*ne of the most satisfying emotions imaginable is the one that tends to engulf me when I am able to show someone something they've never before seen. Actually, it's their excitement that pleases me most. The smile on their face, the wonder—sometimes a look of awe.

It's most fun to show youngsters something new, because they tend to let their feelings be known. And it's easier, too, because young people just plain haven't seen or done everything.

It is my good fortune to have, at this time, six grandchildren and six great-grandchildren as well as innumerable adoptive grandchildren. Obviously, I have many opportunities to show and tell new things. Since virtually all my progeny are "city kids," most, but not necessarily all, the new things I show them have to do with country or farm.

"Gramps! You're not going to be able to talk your way out of it again. Gran says you don't have anything real pressing to do this Saturday, so she agrees it will be a good time for you to take us. We're going and that's it!"

"Whoa! Whoa! Slow down, Randolph. What're you talking about?" Randolph is an impatient young man. So full of vim and vigor even when standing still he seems to be at a full run.

"You're always taking Terry out to 'the lots' and you never have time for us. I want to go hackin' and choppin' and cuttin' and roastin' and it's gonna happen this Saturday." He was talking about hacking brush, chopping and cutting trees and roasting hot dogs at the wooded lots out at the lake.

"All right, already! Since Zena says it's okay, we'll go. But, let's ask Phil Clark, Lloyd Freeman and Chris Meeks if they'd like to go with us." They're some more of my adoptive grandchildren.

"That's who I was talking about when I said 'we'." As it turned out, they all wanted to go. Thought it was a good idea.

First thing Saturday morning I started loading the pickup with things we'd need. Mainly, I tried to find tools they'd never used. Axe, cross cut saw, buck saw, chain saw, limb clippers—and I can't remember what all.

Now, Phil had handled all these tools before. He had been born and raised rural, in Michigan. Matter of fact, he was downright good with all the tools. Strong as an ox, too. Told me he and his brother Dan had been playing hockey since they were little kids. I won't say I didn't believe him, but they both still have all their teeth, if you know what I mean. He's a weight lifter, too. "Pumping iron," they call it.

Another thing I took along was a full picnic basket. Young men eat a lot, especially when they're doing manual labor.

Well, we surely did a lot of hackin' and choppin' and sawin'. You should have seen Randolph and Lloyd trying to handle the crosscut saw. But, they finally got the hang of it.

Before nightfall, we had cleared an area about 50'by 50' leaving the hardwood trees. I never did care all that much for pine trees and those in that particular spot weren't very old anyway.

We had a big fire going all the time. At one point we let it get down to where there was nothing but coals. We buried some potatoes, wrapped in foil, in the embers. Then, we roasted hot dogs.

We had managed to build a makeshift picnic table. Wasn't very fancy, but it served the purpose.

Between bites, Randolph said, "Gramps, this is really living. Let's do it again next Saturday." But, we didn't.

At nightfall, we were tired but fulfilled. Not to mention being over 60 miles from home. And, it was raining.

Now, let me tell you why I wrote this story.

Here in Houston, it's not unusual to see the Goodyear Blimp circling overhead. At different times it will advertise events or things other than Goodyear tires. Great masses of lights seem to cover it and they can flash words or animals and pictures of almost anything. Moving messages or still ones.

You can generally count on the blimp to be on hand for major sporting events as well. You might even get to take a ride in the gondola of the blimp—if you ARE somebody—or if you KNOW somebody or even if you win a ride in a drawing, which they have occasionally.

But, you can see the blimp. Up close. Real close. There's a mammoth hangar on the way to the lots. That's where the Goodyear people store the blimp.

On the way out I asked the boys if they had ever been in the hangar and they all said, "No, but we'd like to." Say no more.

As we drove toward the building, I could see the blimp inside. The hangar doors were open. After we parked and got out, we headed for the entrance. I could see only one person in the office and he was talking on the phone. While I headed in his direction, I urged the boys to walk on up the steps leading into the gondola. And hurry!

They did and my hunch was correct. As soon as the guard spotted them, he hurried out. I managed to stall him for just a little while, but then he started toward them. Even though he had instructions to keep everybody out, he didn't really give the boys the "bum's rush" until they'd had the chance to get the "feel" of riding in a blimp.

What memories of long ago this brought back!

There was a strange, far off, buzzing sound in the air. Mr. Hostetler was standing at the south window looking out, a quizzical look on his face. He seemed to be trying to see toward the east as much as he could.

Suddenly! "First Grade! On your feet! Outside!—Quickly! Now—second grade. Hurry!" And so it went until all eight grades were outside—looking up and toward the south. Only took a couple of minutes.

You talk about incredible—awe—unbelievable! This was almost impossible to imagine or to conceive. Here was this silver-colored, long, fat, cigar shaped apparition, coming from the east and moving toward the west. On the side, in big letters, was painted the word "Goodyear." It was up in the air and seemed to be just floating along. But, of course, it wasn't. There was a long box-shaped car attached underneath and a propeller—maybe two—behind it. We could see people inside the car and they waved to us. The propellers were what was making the humming sound.

We watched until it was out of sight.

Mr. Hostetler told us it was the Goodyear blimp. He had read about it and described to us all he knew about how it was made and how it operated.

That just had to be one of if not *the* most exciting experience of all my school years. I couldn't wait to get home and tell Mom and Dad about it. But, they had seen it, too. It was so big it could be seen for miles.

Mom said, "It was a Dirigible."

Dad said, "No. It was a Zeppelin."

But, I knew it was a blimp. Mr. Hostetler had said so.

40

How Times Change

*A*mos 0. Hostetler was my teacher at Green School in Clay Township, LaGrange County, Indiana, when I attended there in 1929 and 1930. I've always said that some day I was going to write a book about him, but right now, I'd just like to tell a short story about him. He asked me one day if I'd like to go along with him after school to buy a calf. That sounded like a real fun adventure so I said, "Yes, I would." Mr. Hostetler asked my brother Charles to tell my folks, when he got home from school, that Teddy would be late getting home because he and I were going to run an errand.

My dad, whose name was Cecil, always drove a model "T" Ford, but my teacher had a four door model "A".

At this late date in time I can't remember what we talked about as we headed toward US 20 and then on to LaGrange. There's no doubt in my mind that he did a good job of keeping me entertained, maybe by talking about the different cars we were seeing on the highway. The few times Dad let us boys go to town with him, he always took the back road, which was gravel. Route 20 was paved and was an interstate with, even then, a fair number of what seemed like big tractor trailer rigs. There would also have been cars with out-of-state license plates, too, to make conversation about.

When we got to LaGrange, we drove right on through. This seemed like quite a trip because we had already gone some six miles.

It occurred to me that he was going to surprise me and that we were going to Grandpa Todd's farm to get a calf. My grandparents, Joe and Edythe Todd, lived about three miles east and about the same distance south of LaGrange.

But, not so. As we were kind of laboring up the hill east of town past the ever nice-looking Sears farm, he told me that we were going to George Olds' dairy farm. (That hill doesn't seem so steep any more, but I remember our struggling to make it then.) George Olds had a beautiful farm and buildings. Way back off the road and I especially remember the big silos.

Mr. Olds came out as we drove up. When we got out of the car he extended a hand to Mr. Hostetler and said, "What can I do for you?" I don't remember that he knew Mr. Hostetler, but when I was introduced to him he asked if I was one of Cecil Woodworth's boys and was Sylvia my mother. I told him that I was their youngest. He said he and his wife knew my folks well. I also soon found out he had a daughter a little younger than me and a boy a couple years older.

Mr. Olds again asked what brought us to his farm. Mr. Hostetler said, "I've been told that because you have so many dairy cattle you also have lots of calves. I'm also told that you don't have much use for the bull calves. Is that true?"

"That's very true. As a matter of fact, right this very minute I have a five-day-old male calf that one of my biggest Jersey cows presented me with. Do you want to see it?"

With that we went into the barn to have a look. The cow and calf were in a kind of fenced-in area about ten foot square. The cow was beautiful and the calf was a big one. It was having its supper when we came in.

Mr. Olds explained that for a few days after calving the cow gives very rich milk for the benefit of the newborn calf. But, the dairy is not allowed to include this milk with their regular dairy milk. For that reason they keep the calf with its mother during the time it's giving this rich milk.

He also told us that there was not much market for calves this age and so in some instances, he just does away with them.

"How much do you want for it?" Mr. Hostetler asked. He liked the looks of it and it was indeed a real beauty, tan and off white.

Mr. Olds' reply was, "You can have it for nothing, but you'll have to keep it for a few weeks and feed it milk so it'll keep growing for a while. They're not too good to eat at this age."

Mr. Hostetler had a small farm on the west side of Rainbow Lake and a couple of cows, so he had the milk as well as plenty of room and pasture. However, Mr. Hostetler never wanted "something for nothing."

"No, I don't want it for nothing. How much do you want?"

Mr. Olds' answer was, "Well, if you feel that way about it, give me fifty cents."

"That's a bargain." Whereupon Mr. Hostetler got his snap pocketbook out and handed Mr. Olds a shiny fifty-cent piece.

I can still see Mr. Hostetler squatting down and wrapping his arms around all four of the calf's legs and carrying him to the car. At the time I was worried about his getting his blue coat sweater dirty, but he didn't. Mr. Olds helped put the calf into a gunny sack, then they tied the top of the sack around the calf's neck.

I opened the back door and Mr. Hostetler put the calf on the floor between the front and the back seat. After we closed the door it didn't take a minute for the calf to get out of the gunny sack and onto the back seat on all fours.

As we drove away, waving goodbye to Mr. Olds and Alice and Bill, the calf licked me right in the face.

It was an enjoyable time and I'm sure Mr. Hostetler could tell how really happy he had made me as he dropped me off at home.

What chance would there be today of buying a 40 to 50-pound calf for fifty cents? Shucks, you can't even buy a baby chick for that!

How times change.

41

The Buck Sheep

*Z*ena, that's my wife, loves to travel. We both do. And we travel quite a lot. But, there's more than one way to satisfy your craving for travel. We watch western shows on TV.

Many's the time we've traveled on a covered wagon with "Wagon Train," galloped across the Kansas prairie with Matt Dillon and Chester on "Gunsmoke," or tried to help Rowdy stop a stampede in the middle of the night on "Rawhide."

One of our favorites is "Bonanza." That's got to be one really big ranch. It has everything. Farmland, apple orchards, orange groves, big plains, rolling hills and mountains. There are lush valleys, streams as big as rivers, lakes. You name it. Bonanza's got it.

There's a certain amount of violence in some of these movies, but no foul language or explicit bedroom scenes and the good guys always win. We watch them in order to enjoy the scenery and to imagine being able to re-live some of the frontier times.

Several years ago we experienced the pleasure of spending eight days at the Wickenberg Inn. This is a dude ranch out in the desert a few miles from Wickenberg, Arizona.

It was a much more pleasurable and memorable experience than we had dreamed it could be. I highly recommend it. They featured horseback riding, tennis and food. Not having much experience at tennis, my boy Terry and I indulged ourselves in food, swimming and horseback riding.

Zena went riding with us once and I've got pictures to prove it, but she didn't get any further than the corral. Everybody was mounted on their horses, including the three of us. But, there was a holdup of some sort. Zena's horse became impatient and decided another mouthful of hay would be in order, so he just casualty walked over to the hay stack and started munching away.

Zena didn't know what to do and she was frightened. She couldn't seem to control the horse. Somehow, the horse seemed to sense that she was afraid and he just plain took over. One of the cowboys walked over to where she and the horse were to try to calm her down. No way! Zena had had all the fun she could enjoy. The cowboy helped her off the horse and she went back to the bungalow. Afterward she marveled at how strong he was. Riding lessons were available, the cowboy told her. She said, "Thanks, but no thanks."

Terry and I really enjoyed riding out through the desert and even into the foothills. Just like in the movies, we rode through mesquite and purple sage and dry river beds. We scared up jackrabbits, lizards and one time saw a snake all coiled up. We trotted and galloped and thought, "Eat your heart out, John Wayne."

The hayride, then steaks broiled over open mesquite fires were a prelude to looking up through cloudless and smogless skies at a zillion twinkling stars, while the cowboys played their guitars and sang western songs.

Early, early in the morning, we'd peer through the curtained windows to watch the quail and rabbits just outside, scratching and nibbling and making the noises that wild creatures make. Then, always, there were two roadrunners on top of the thatched roof covering the spectator bench alongside the tennis court. We'd rush to put on our clothes so we could get outside in time to look off to the east and watch the sunrise. Absolutely spectacular! Truly one of the most outstanding of God's creations.

On a recent segment of "Bonanza," Little Joe and Hoss Cartwright were tracking a big buck sheep. They were in the hills and there was a lot of snow. It seemed the buck sheep always knew where they were, but Little Joe and Hoss couldn't keep track of the buck sheep.

Reminded me of something that happened to me on the Black Walnut Farm when I was a kid.

To or from school, it was shorter for us boys to cut through Grandma's farm. On this particular afternoon, Wayne and Charles walked home on the road. I chose to take the shortcut. We could look out the window of the school house and see Grandma's house across the road. All I had to do was walk up the driveway, climb the fence into the barnyard, then after climbing out the other side, I crossed two fields and I was home.

At this point in time, Grandma had a flock of sheep grazing in her apple orchard. There was a wire fence separating the orchard from the road and a wire fence along the adjoining field. Yet, the fence along the driveway and the lane on the fourth side had a rail fence. I'd guess it was about four feet high.

Lots of things will distract little boys and the sheep distracted me. Especially, the big buck sheep. Every flock of sheep includes a buck sheep. Mostly, they're not friendly.

I climbed up on the rail fence next to the lane. I was in full view of the house, but I didn't see Grandma anywhere. The buck sheep separated himself from the flock and slowly walked over to within about six feet of the fence. He looked up at me and went "Baa-a-a-" in what sounded like a deep baritone voice. I answered in what he probably thought was a boy soprano voice. What he was telling me was "Get on your way, boy!" Since I was safely on the fence I wasn't scared, so I went "Baa-a-a-a" right back at him. Matter of fact, we did it at each other several times. I thought it was great fun, but he finally turned and walked slowly back to the flock. Like he was bored.

Dad had trimmed the apple trees and stacked the limbs on one big pile. I decided to get on top of this brush pile. I climbed down from the rail fence and made a run for it. The buck seemed to start toward me then changed his mind. From my safe perch, I started taunting him. "Baa-a-a-a-a, Baa-a-a-a-a-" over and over again. He didn't pay any attention. I was kind of jumping up and down when all of a sudden a rabbit ran out of his hiding place in the brush pile. I took off after this new attraction as he headed for the rail fence. He went under the fence and I went flying over the fence with an assist from the big buck sheep.

You see, he had been keeping a careful eye on me and anticipated what I would do when the rabbit ran out. I'm here to tell you, he moved fast, because he caught up to me just before I got to the fence. He bucked me so hard in the seat of the pants that I cleared the fence. I wonder if he was working in cahoots with that rabbit. You suppose?

There never was much of an indication that Grandma Woodworth had a sense of humor. However, a few days after this episode, which I sure didn't tell anybody about, Dad came home from town with a story for Mom. I wasn't supposed to be overhearing this, but he had stopped at Grandma's on his way home and she told him, between laughs, about what had happened. Mom and Dad laughed about it, too. Finally, Mom said, "Aren't you going to punish him?"

"Naah. I think the old buck sheep did a good enough job of it."

42

My Friend, Nedra

$\mathcal{N}$edra was a grade ahead of me in school. That didn't make any difference to me because I was taller. Actually, she was kind of petite. Small. Even though she was a farm girl, she was light complexioned. For sure, she was pretty. One of a kind, Nedra was.

After grade school, I don't remember ever seeing her again. More's the pity, for I'm sure she became a fine lady with a loving husband and three or four doting children.

On the rare occasions I get back "up home," I usually pass by the farm where she was born and raised. It still says "Earl Norris" on the barn. The big red brick house is still there, and occupied, I think, by Milbourn Norris, her brother.

My imagination conjures up a big orchard extending from the house and barn all the way to road 20. But, it's only my imagination. There is no orchard and probably never was. I think there should be, though.

Somehow, my memory of her has more to do with the old Bethel Church than with Green School, though we attended at the same time. My family and I didn't go to church every Sunday. But, there were special Sundays we tried never to miss.

"Children's Day" was one of those. Naturally, it was intended to encourage the children to become more interested in Jesus and the Bible as well as the church. Jesus wanted us to come to him, the teacher said. "Suffer the little children to come unto me and forbid them not, for of such is the Kingdom of Heaven." It was a convincing point and we responded.

Merril Eaton was the music director, but my memory says his wife Vera was the Sunday School teacher.

They lived on the nice looking farm adjacent to the Saylor School. I remember the buildings were well kept and seemed always to have been freshly painted. Their farm wasn't more than a mile from the Bethel Church.

The entertainment, or program, was put on by the children on Children's Day. Supervised by Merril Eaton, of course. Practice! Practice! Practice! "Practice makes perfect," Mr. Eaton used to say. And, he wanted all of us to be perfect. For at least two weeks before Children's Day, Mom had to take us—me and my brothers and sisters—to the church for practice.

Ordinarily, we only went to the church on Sunday mornings. Going in the evening and then returning sometimes in the dark was a whole new experience. For one thing, when we had a nice clear moonlit night, the moon furnished us with more light to drive by than did the headlamps. Mom said, in righteous indignation, "I know why they measure light by 'candle power.' The headlights on this confounded Model T could easily be replaced by one good candle." Wel-l-l-l, they were a little better than that. In truth, though, after dark Mom would pull over to the side of the road and stop when we met a car from the other direction.

If the weather was at all bad, Mom would just practice with us at home. The "Old Reed Organ" sounded better than the piano at the church, anyway. Only catch was, I didn't have my partner to practice with. You see—I was going to sing a duet with my friend, Nedra Norris. l argued it just wasn't the same, practicing singing by myself. "Hush up, Teddy, and get ready to sing. I may not have time later." Mom always ended the argument by saying, "Nedra probably won't be there anyway."

She was most likely right. Earl Norris and his boys always worked hard and late. That's the only way any of the farmers were able to "keep their heads above water." And he did.

Two other participants in the "Children's Day" entertainment were Charles and Evelyn Stewart.

The Stewarts lived in a house on the south side of "Palmers Hill." That's the hill my Dad's Model T Ford had a running battle with. Many's the time we just plain couldn't get up enough power to get over the crest of the hill. Sometimes, when we couldn't quite make it to the top, Mom would turn the steering wheel sharply and let it roll backward. Then she'd quickly straighten out the steering wheel and press the reverse pedal.

That's right! She'd back to the top of the hill. Somehow, the T Model had more power in reverse and at low speed than it had in low forward gear.

The Model T was a good car if it was properly maintained. Couldn't be beat as a "mudder." It seemed to enjoy deep ruts in the road. Had something to do with the big narrow wheels and tires.

Mr. Stewart didn't have any trouble negotiating "Palmer Hill" with his Chevrolet. Matter of fact, he used to challenge Ma to race. I think he had four children and there were always that many of us in our car. We kids would "egg" them on. Mom was a good sport and so was Mr. Stewart—so—away they'd go.

Compared to the speed of today's cars, they didn't go very fast. Probably not more than forty miles an hour. Considering that Dad never drove over 25 miles an hour, it seemed real fast to us. Mr. Stewart would always win because he didn't have a problem with the hill. He'd be turning into his driveway by the time we cleared the top of the hill. The racing was a real thrill for us—and it was Mom's and our secret from Dad. He never knew.

But, all the practicing and driving back and forth was worth it. "Children's Day" attendance was as close to 100 percent as we ever had. The children all wanted to be there, and so we brought some terrific pressure to bear on our parents to come.

I don't know that any of us had what is known as natural talent, but Mr. Eaton knew his "stuff" and he got good results. By the day of the program, we were good. Very good. Merrill Eaton saw to it.

On the big day, the yard was full of cars and the church was full of children and their parents and friends, all wanting to hear the young ones perform.

First were the teenagers. Solos—duets—trios—and quartets. Beautiful, very good. Then the younger ones.

Naturally, the song I remember the best was sung by Nedra Norris and Ted Woodworth. That's me.

"Angry words, Oh let them never,
From the tongue, unbridled slip.
Check the heart's best impulse ever,
Ere they touch and soil the lips.
Love one another—thus saith the Savior.
Children obey their parents blessed commands.
Love one another—thus saith the Savior.
Children obey their blessed commands."

There was more, but that's all I remember. We were last on the program. When we finished, there was tremendous applause. Not for just our duet, but for all the young singers.

How grand it would be if we would all practice the words of this song, "Angry words, Oh, let them never."

43

With One Arm Tied Behind My Back!

*I*n turning the pages of a sportsman's calendar to September, I was again taken back in time. Back to when I walked to school either with my brothers or by myself.

It's probably just my imagination, but it seemed as though my brothers and I didn't look at various things the same way. For instance, to me, birds were a thing of beauty. To admire. To listen to. My brothers thought they were to throw rocks at. I don't remember their ever hitting one, but it wasn't for lack of trying.

Also the rocks. I used to polish and save them. Many had interesting shapes as well as colors. To my brothers, rocks were for testing marksmanship. About halfway between our house and the road turning toward Green School, there was a big stone pile. It was along the fence at the very back of Black Walnut Farm. Years before, when Dad or one of his brothers was plowing or dragging or whatever, they'd always stop and pick up any rock that interrupted their work. Then, they'd throw them along the fence at the end of the field. Dad quipped one time about our farm, "This farm produces more rocks than it does corn. I get maybe 25 bushels of corn to the acre and about 60 bushels of rocks." Maybe they did break a lot of plow points, but I always saw rocks as something created for a reason. There just had to be a good use for them.

In the fall, the trees and bushes are breathtakingly beautiful in Indiana. The sumac bushes, sassafras and maple trees, and the bittersweet vines all provide a veritable kaleidoscope of colors.

The sight of rabbits scurrying out of hiding places, squirrels in the walnut trees alongside the road on the Black Walnut Farm, the crow of the ringneck pheasants as they took flight—all these things I got to enjoy as I walked to school in the fall.

Many of the simple things of life are pleasant to recall, as testified to in a nice letter I received recently from Loretta (Beachy) Herschberger, who lives in Kokomo. She writes, in part:

"I love to receive my Friday's paper to read your letter on the back page. It reminds me that you don't have to write about lovely maidens who suddenly become millionaires and inherit a seaside villa or maybe about a tall dark sinister stranger who stalks her dreams.

"You just write truthful things that happened to you and it's interesting reading now because times change.

"Everyone likes to think back to their childhood and remember it as 'the good old days.' When age and time erase the hard times you endured; the dust, sweat, spankings, cows that kicked you as you milked them—the list is endless.

"Yes, our minds are programmed to remember the good times. And forget the bad times. And it's a good thing, too. What woman would have two children if all she could remember was the pain of the first one?"

Now, doesn't she have a real flair for putting words together?

Meanwhile, back on the road to school, it started to rain and I still had a ways to go. Hurry! Hurry! It wasn't supposed to rain, according to Dad, but it did. Most of the kids, many of whom had arrived in the school hack, were already inside the school. High and dry. Not me. I was soaked through and through. Probably should have stayed inside at noon recess, but I didn't and I caused trouble. Again.

LeRoy Combs was in the same grade as my brother Wayne, so he was quite a bit bigger than me. His sister, Hazel, was a grade behind me. His brother, Ray, had already gotten all the "book larnin'" he felt he needed, so he didn't go to school.

By noon recess the sun was shining. I guess, maybe I thought I could get dried off by being outdoors in the sun. Anyway, LeRoy started pestering me. Said I had looked like a "drownded dawg" when I came to school that morning, and didn't look all that much better now. Wayne took offense.

But, then, he and LeRoy were always looking for a reason to wrestle. LeRoy and Wayne were both tall, gangly, rawboned country boys. They had wrestled before and it looked like it was going to happen again.

"Ah never meynt the kiyud no horm, an iffii ye take a step tords me I'm fixin tuh clean yor plaow."

147

LeRoy hadn't lost his Kentucky accent.

"You'll clean my plow?" Wayne yelled! "You've never seen the day you could get the best of me! Why, I can whip you with one arm tied behind my back."

"Yer on. Sum uh yew boahs tah his orm behint his bake." And they did.

Now, these two never hit each other with their fists. Just wrestled. And they surely did wrestle this time. Real serious like.

Wayne never lost his confidence, but it turned out to be more of a job than he had reckoned for. LeRoy was sure he could beat him, especially since he had one arm tied behind his back. Two or three times, Wayne managed to grab LeRoy in such a way that he was able to trip him. Then he'd pounce on top of him. LeRoy kept managing to wiggle out from under, but he was beginning to have some doubts as to how this was going to turn out.

Then it happened. Because it had rained that morning, the ditch along the road in front of the school was about half full of water. Wayne got LeRoy down in the water. That was too much. LeRoy gave up.

The other boys untied Wayne's arm and the two of them shook hands—friends again. That should have been it. But, it wasn't.

The bell rang. Time to go back into the schoolhouse. Amos met them at the door. Uh—Mr. Hostetler, that is. Both were soaking, dripping wet. Not only that, they were muddy and LeRoy had most of his shirt torn off. No way was he going to let them in his nice clean school room.

Mr. Hostetler didn't ask any questions. He just said, "Do you two hooligans think you can find your way home without getting into any more trouble?"

"Yes, Sir!" they chimed in unison.

"Then, get on home and change your clothes. See how quickly you can get back here. On second thought, today is Friday. Don't come back until Monday morning."

Expelled! For half a day. How about that? Wait a minute! They got to go home because they were wet. I was wet when I got to school, but he never said a word. Doesn't seem fair. Oh, well! Win some—lose some.

44

Keep Your Eye on the Ball

*D*uring my lifetime, I've heard many an "old saying." Dad was especially proficient at quoting them. I think he must have read a book about old sayings that went clear back to the year one and then he never forgot any of them.

My children claim that I've been known to spout old sayings and then present them as "Woodworth Truisms." I'd like to think I come up with a new one, now and again. Fact is, I like to poke fun at truisms as well as quote them.

For instance, to be successful in life you must:

"Keep your eye on the ball,
Keep your ear to the ground,
and Keep your nose to the grindstone."
Right? Sure, but let's see you work from that position.

How about, "The early bird gets the worm." But, who likes worms?

Anyway, it wasn't Dad that inspired this story. No, once again it was my long ago teacher, Amos 0. Hostetler. I have a lot of things to thank him for and I'm most assuredly not the only one who does.

It's true that from time to time, Mr. Hostetler was guilty of not explaining in sufficient detail one of his old sayings. In some instances we understood his meaning at once. Then again, it might have taken hours or weeks, and on occasion, years, to gain the full benefit from his teachings. Sometimes, he was deep.

In the situation at hand, he was talking directly to me. Nobody else. Not that I was the only one expected to learn from his comments. No, the whole team was supposed to benefit and they did.

As I have reported before, I wasn't a very proficient athlete. To put it mildly and honestly, I had two left feet and was clumsy. My ungainliness lasted at least through the third grade.

Mr. Hostetler didn't have to put up with me in the first grade, because he wasn't teaching at Green School that year, and I attended Saylor School in the fourth year. So, he was my teacher in the second and third grades and then I was back again for the fifth grade.

In this instance, I was in the third grade. Since I was fairly worthless on the baseball team itself, Mr. Hostetler, who was always in charge, had decided I should be the umpire. A prestigious assignment, I felt.

Now, it's true I knew the rudimentary rules of baseball, but I wasn't too well-versed in some of the finer points. Mr. Hostetler was very well aware of this. I was about to receive some lasting instructions.

Captains had been designated and two teams chosen. I was not among those selected by either captain. Amos had volunteered to fill the position of catcher for both teams.

There was no boy in our school who would have made a better catcher than Mr. Hostetler. For a fact, no matter what position he chose to play, none of us could have done as well, let alone better. He was a natural born athlete, if there is such a thing.

It was really something to watch him pitch or throw somebody out at any base. And catching? That's what I'm wanting to talk about.

In the game of baseball, it's imperative that every player keeps his eye on the ball. The only time a player is even remotely forgiven for losing track of the ball is when a high fly puts the ball in direct line with the sun when an outfielder is trying to catch it. And even then—well—he's still supposed to keep his eye on the ball.

Bob Noel was pitching. He learned early to wind up—put his left foot up in the air—and throw the ball a mile a minute—early in his career. Smack! Into the catcher's mitt.

But, wait a minute. Amos had caught the ball high and outside, but almost quicker than the eye could follow, he'd yanked it back into the strike zone! What to do? Mr. Hostetler held the ball in his catcher's mitt right in the middle of the strike zone.

He slowly turned his head toward me and said, "Well, Ted?"

Real quick like, I said, "Strike?"

That's when the lesson began, for all of us. Mr. Hostetler brought the game to a screeching halt in spite of the fact it had just begun. "No use in doing anything, unless you're going to do it right." That was probably another of his "old sayings."

After both teams had assembled as close to home plate as they could, Mr. Hostetler started in on me. "All right, Ted! Did you see a strike or didn't you?"

"Well, er, what I saw, or rather what I thought I saw, was, er, it was a ball. But, then, suddenly you were holding it right in the middle of the strike zone. So, I called it a strike."

What I was really thinking was, you're the teacher and you pulled the ball into the strike zone, so you wanted it to be a strike. I'd better not go against your will or I'm in trouble. I'll just call it a strike.

"No! Ted. No! That's not the way it works. Keep your eye on the ball and call it the way you see it. Not the way it appears to be. The pitch was a ball. You saw it right the first time. Don't change your mind, if you're convinced you're right, no matter what."

It was a valuable lesson and we never forgot it.

"Things are not always the way they seem to be," he said. And on with our education.

45

Saylor School's Baseball Wonder

I received a letter the other day indicating country boys' attitudes toward school haven't changed just a whole lot since I was a boy. Maybe a little, but not much. According to the letter, it seems as though both Adam Wayne and Andrew Maynard Yoder III prefer softball to any of their other subjects. Sounds perfectly normal to me. When I went to Green School, my favorite subject was recess and often the activity was baseball.

Not too many years ago, I used to play a lot of catch with my son Terry. And we used to join in baseball games at picnics and such. But not any more. My bones are too brittle.

I saw something the other day made me think of this story I'm going to write, soon as I can get started on it. There was this girls' softball team playing against this other all-girl team. Now, let me tell you! This pitcher was something else. She wound up and let go with the fastest underhand pitch I've ever seen. Man or boy. Almost the instant the ball left her hand, you heard it smack as it hit the catcher's mitt. And, at the same time, the umpire was hollering "stee-e-rike three" and the batter was heading for the bench. Amazing! That ball was moving like greased lightning. The batter couldn't see it, let alone hit it.

Mr. Hostetler would have said it was unladylike. I don't know, maybe he's changed. But, I doubt it. Amos was pretty set in his attitude about how a young lady should conduct herself. He strongly believed ladies were the "weaker vessels" and should act and be treated accordingly.

Girls playing softball just sort of goes along with the women's lib movement, however. Then there's women's basketball teams in competition. They get rough, too. Speaking of rough, "ladies" roller skating derbies are positively unbelievable. Wow! You can't believe how they knock each other around. And ladies "mud-wrestling?" What next? Some of the world's fastest runners and swimmers are women. And tennis players! Their ability and stamina are far superior to most men. And golf? It's hard to believe how far some of them can hit a golf ball. "A country mile," as the feller says.

Well, anyway, when I was in grade school, Mr. Hostetler would never have allowed the girls to participate in the games that are traditionally played by boys. Even if he would have allowed it, I can't picture girls such as Nedra Norris, Naomi Hooley, Lois Mishler or Margaret Doney wanting to play some of the rough games that boys play.

We had some good baseball players at Green School. For instance, my brothers Wayne and Charles, Tom Bradley, Milbourn Norris, Byron and Roy Foltz, Ernest Gooch and more. By the third grade, Clarence Seaney and Bob Noel were as good as the older boys. Most of the rest of us were just "warm bodies."

Wait, there were some others I've almost forgotten. There was Marion Atwater. I think he was a "lefty." And Art Schemerhorn and John Doney. Can't leave out Elmer and Vernon Neff or Paul Bradley, either. After thinking about it for a while, I guess most all of the boys were better ball players than I was. But, I made a good vocal enthusiastic spectator.

I did get to play, though. Mr. Hostetler saw to it that all the boys got to play, no matter how inept they were. "How else will you learn?" he'd say. And I guess he was right, because I did learn to play and to really enjoy it.

The story I started out to tell involved another one-room school in the same township. Saylor School. Word had come to us that they had a first class baseball team. Mr. Hostetler thought we had a good team too, so he challenged them to a game.

Elizabeth Neely was their teacher and she was the first one off the Saylor School "hack" when it arrived. Every kid in their school was on the "hack." (Now we would call it a bus.) Excitement and anticipation had been running high at both schools. There was lots of shouting and yelling of greetings as they unloaded.

In short order our team was on the playing field. Since we were the home team, it would be their first "at bat." For the life of me, I can't remember who our pitcher was, but it was probably Bob Noel. From early on, he was really good.

Since there were no benches or spectator bleachers, everybody was forced to stand or else they sat on the ground. Of course, each team stood separate from the other students who did a lot of cheering for their respective teams.

As their batters were sort of standing in line for their turn at bat, it suddenly and spontaneously dawned on the Green School students that one of the Saylor School players was a girl. A girl! Playing baseball! We'd never heard of such a thing, so naturally there commenced loud hooting and hollering until her turn at bat. Then it stopped.

She stepped up to the plate and promptly slammed the first pitch clear across the road—across the fence—and into George Doney's corn field. Home run! Saylor School's baseball "wonder" had smacked one of the longest home runs any of us had ever seen.

A real first class "tom-boy", and no doubt about it. The reason we didn't realize she was a girl was she wore "overalls" and a shirt instead of a dress. She also had her hair tucked under a cap just like the ones some of the boys wore.

She was also an outstanding second baseman and, as it turned out, she wasn't the only "wonder" on their team. The one I remember best was Arthur "Art" Kern. I'll tell you what, he had a wicked fast ball and a mean curve.

I later got to know some of their other players' names. There was Wayne and Winford "Windy" Lewis and Jim Riggsby. And then Charles Parsons and Bruce Slack. I got to know all these boys later, when I attended Saylor School for a year.

Oh, yes! June Parsons, "Chuck" Parsons' sister, was Saylor School's baseball "wonder."

46

I Wish I Was Adopted

We started school together in the first grade and we graduated together from high school. Then I never saw him again.

We were friends during that time and I'm sorry we lost track of each other. I'm kind of glad that he never knew how much I envied him. He was one of the nicest boys I ever knew and it would have embarrassed him.

There were six children in my family and he was an only child. We both lived on farms and attended a one-room school where all eight grades learned their three "R's."

One day he asked me if I'd like to come home with him and spend the night. That sounded like a splendid idea to me for several reasons. One reason was that he was a well-liked and popular boy and I was flattered that he had asked me. Another was that I was just sure that he had a lot of toys. Most of our toys were ones that my brothers had made. Yet another reason was that he lived a lot further from the school than I did and so he got to ride the school bus. I had never done that because we only lived a little over a mile from the school and so my brothers and sisters and I always had to walk to and from school, winter and summer.

Anyway, that night I asked my Mom if I could go home with him after school the next day. She thought it would be nice for me, too. The next morning she took more than the usual care to see that I was dressed "fitten," like making sure there were no holes in my socks.

We had a great time at his house and I was really impressed. He had a bicycle and a wagon and smaller toys like cars and trucks. We played with jigsaw puzzles and other games that night.

He even had his own room, with a closet, and the nicest clothes I could remember ever having seen. He even had more than one pair of shoes! The things in his drawers were all folded up nice and neat. The whole room was clean and tidy.

Included among his shoes were a pair of baseball shoes with real cleats. You see, his really big love was baseball.

His dad had nailed a bushel basket to the barn door and he spent hours throwing at it with a baseball. He said it was to improve his pitching ability and he was really good. He could put it into the basket almost every time, no matter how hard he threw it.

I'm nearly certain that he was the school's pitcher by the time he was in the third grade.

The school picture that was taken when we were in either the second or third grade revealed a clue to his love of the game.

The schoolbus was used for the backdrop. In those days, a school bus was called a "hack." The hack driver and the teacher and the taller students stood with their backs to the hack. In the next row, the next taller students knelt and then in the front row the littlest ones were seated.

He was in the front row. He really stood out because of the bulges in his front pockets. In each was a baseball. In addition to his being a good student, it seemed as though he ate, slept and breathed baseball. Weather permitting, we ate our lunch outside. He had one of those nice lunch buckets that had a thermos jug in the top. His mom always filled it with hot chocolate or soup of some kind. Without fail he had two sandwiches spread with real butter and a generous amount of peanut butter. Along with that he had cookies and a piece of fruit or a jar of canned fruit.

I've got to tell you about the sandwiches. They were made from store bought sandwich bread. The slices were square. His mother cut the sandwiches from one corner to the other, making two triangles. I thought that was really aristocratic. But, he almost never ate all of both sandwiches. When that happened he gave away the part he didn't eat. I always tried to sit next to him and many times I was rewarded with his generosity. I promise you, I was a grateful recipient, because my lunch was often quite skimpy. The night I stayed with him, his mother packed me the best lunch I could ever remember having.

When I told my mother about his nice room and clothes and that she fixed us hot chocolate when we were ready for bed, she told me something I hadn't known and didn't really understand. She told me that he was adopted. My instant response was, "I wish I was adopted!"

She then told me that his parents had adopted him when he was a tiny baby. They loved him very much and were able to do things for him that my folks weren't able to do for me because there were six of us. "But that doesn't mean we don't love you as much as they love him," Mom said. Her saying that made me realize that there is little difference in the love felt and shown by parents whether their children be adopted or natural.

That hasn't stopped me from wondering if he realized how fortunate he was. I have no doubt that he made his parents very proud. I did find out that he graduated from college and was able to pursue his love of baseball and later basketball in that he became a high school coach.

Most adopted children are very blessed. To their parents they are special. Virtually without fail, their adoptive parents really wanted them and in many cases went to extremes to get them. Their love has no end.

47

"Who Bought the Piano, Amos?"

*T*his story is about one of my favorite subjects—Amos Hostetler. I remember him well. As it turns out, my memory has stored things about him that he isn't able to recall.

For example, his navy blue coat sweater. He wore that sweater almost daily for six years. He did! It's in my memory bank. But, he doesn't remember it.

Another example: his black shoes. As far as I know, he wore the same pair of shoes for the same six years.

One more: rubbers. Just barely covered his shoes. Always wore them when he went outside. Probably, that's why his shoes didn't wear out.

When Mr. Hostetler came to school in the morning, driving his black, two seater, Model A Ford, the minute he stepped inside the door, off came the sweater. He had his own private hook to hang up his sweater—or coat and sweater—and black hat—if it was winter time. Then off came the rubbers.

Now then, when he left the school house, even to make a quick trip to the privy house out in back, he always reversed the procedure. He'd put on the rubbers and the coat sweater, but not necessarily his hat.

I remember! He was a creature of habit and neatness was one of his habits.

Over the years, Mr. Hostetler told us a lot about himself. And about his habits, his wife, his children, his home life in general. We appreciated that. Made us feel closer to him.

One time he did an absolute no-no. He came to school unshaven! I never knew but that he did it deliberately, just to illustrate a point about "habits."

In the "old days" when homes—especially farm homes—had no bathroom, it was customary to bathe completely only once a week. Mr. Hostetler ordinarily put on all his clothes, except his

158

shirt, before washing, then shaving, then lastly brushing his teeth. He had beautiful white teeth. It was obvious he brushed them regularly.

On this particular morning, something distracted him. He brushed his teeth first! Without any hesitation, he then put on his shirt and sat down to the breakfast table with his family. As he put it, "Everybody was still half asleep, so nobody noticed I hadn't shaved. After giving a prayer of thanks for the food we were about to enjoy, I hurriedly ate my breakfast, put on my sweater and rubbers and headed for the car. And here I am. Unshaven!" There was no doubt about it, because his beard was black and as heavy as my Dad's. And that was heavy. "A routine," that's what he called it. "You form a habit of routine. I broke it and you see what happened."

A heavy percentage of the lessons taught us by Mr. Hostetler came from the Bible rather than from conventional text books. Now, I don't mean to imply Mr. Hostetler taught Bible classes, or lessons, at Green School. I mean his teaching was Bible-based. Like, his wanting us to form good habits.

One of his favorite sayings was, "It's just as easy to form good habits as it is to form bad habits."

He encouraged us to brush our teeth and to keep our bodies clean. "After all," he'd say, "cleanliness is next to Godliness." Neatness counted heavily with him, too.

"When you grow up, don't use tobacco or alcohol. They're harmful to your body." Certainly, the use of tobacco has been proven to be very detrimental to good health. Many have died of cancer and other diseases related to the use of tobacco. Excessive use of alcohol has caused innumerable and tragic problems, as well.

Amos Hostetler was a good, conscientious teacher. He truly had our best interests at heart and earnestly wanted us to get a good education. I wouldn't want to leave the impression he didn't want us to learn about the Bible. Quite the contrary. On Monday morning, each student was required to quote, from memory, one Bible verse. And, we did it. More than once, when somebody had failed or forgotten to memorize a verse, they'd fall back on trusty old, "Jesus wept." We had no prayer in school. Nor, for that

159

matter, was there a "flag salute" or "Pledge of Allegiance." These things came later when patriotic fervor was running high at the beginning of World War II.

At the time Mr. Hostetler was teaching us such things as sportsmanship, honesty, consideration for each other and not losing our tempers, I wonder if there wasn't something deeper? He was probably trying to teach us what the Bible refers to as the fruitage of the spirit, which is love, joy, peace, long-suffering, kindness, goodness, faith, mildness, self-control. Wouldn't this be a wonderful world in which to live if everybody exercised the fruitage of the spirit?

Amos Hostetler seldom did anything by accident. He was quick-witted and definitely had a sense of humor. One of his great joys was singing, and he was good. I heard him sing on several different occasions.

Maybe it has changed, but back in those days, there was no piano in the Mennonite Church where Mr. Hostetler was a member. He was not only a member, but he was one of the ministers. Still is, for that matter.

Even though there was no piano at the church and all singing was done *a cappella*, Mr. Hostetler liked the sound of a piano. Therefore, he set out to find one. A timing fork was all right to use to start off the singing at church, but he wanted a piano in his home for the enjoyment of his family. The search was on.

First, he tried Caton's Funeral and Furniture Store. There were no music stores, especially in small towns, so pianos were sold at furniture stores. I guess it is a piece of furniture, at that.

Amos had never shopped for a piano and he was in for a rude awakening. The price of a new piano was so high he couldn't even afford to buy the stool let alone the piano. That was it for new pianos.

Watching the "For Sale" ads in the local newspaper, the Standard, didn't produce any results until—suddenly—there it was. A chance. A used piano was included in the household furniture to be sold at a farm auction sale.

'Mr. Hostetler stopped by the farm to examine the piano. He had attended enough auction sales to be aware of the unwritten auction law—"*caveat emptor*"—which is Latin for "let the buyer beware." After satisfying himself the piano was a good one, he made a mental note as to how much he could afford to pay for it. He told us all this on a Friday. The sale was the next day.

All week end, Charles, Wayne and I kept wondering if the Hostetlers were the proud new owners of a piano. We wanted them to get it because we had so much enjoyment from our Crown organ. Monday finally came, but Mr. Hostetler wouldn't answer our insistent questioning—until school took up. "Who bought the piano, Amos?" This is the story he told us:

Mrs. Hostetler had looked forward with keen anticipation. "Our very own piano. How fine!" But, Saturday, when he pulled into the driveway after the sale with nothing on his small trailer but some tools, his wife was most disappointed. No piano.

"Who bought the piano, Amos?" she asked.

"I didn't know the man," was his reply.

Mrs. Hostetler didn't say another word. Just dejectedly went about her household duties. The children were very quiet, too. They had also wanted their home to have a piano.

Then, "Look! Look! There's a stake truck driving in and it has a piano in the back!" The children and their mother were all shouting at once. "I can't believe it! For the first time in our married life, you didn't tell me the truth, Amos. You said you didn't know the man who bought the piano."

"But, I didn't know him. For one thing, I didn't know I'd pay as much as I did for it. There were others who wanted it and they ran the price up. I paid half again as much as I had planned to pay. Another thing, somebody who really knew how played the piano before the sale and I hadn't realized how beautiful it would sound. Besides, I knew you wanted it and my heart was anxious to please you. Our heart is the seat of motivation."

"So you see, my dearest one, I didn't know the man who bought the piano."

There it was again. A lesson from the Bible. This time, likely Jeremiah 17:9 which reads, "The heart is more treacherous than anything else and is desperate. Who can know it?"

That was a deep lesson, but we understood. Sort of . . . .

161

48

If You're Innocent, Don't Plead Guilty

*A*college-educated psychologist would have a field day with this story. It concerns discipline. Amos Hostetler didn't have a degree, but he practiced psychology, nonetheless. In my case, child psychology. Amos was our teacher at Green School. He taught the first through the eighth grades. Kids from six to sixteen. We had to call him Mr. Hostetler and that was proper. Then, without question, one respected his elders and he was four times as old as I was.

I should be able to get by calling him Amos now because he's not quite half ag'in as old as I am. I'm gaining on him. Percentage wise. Only recently I discovered that he had steadily progressed from country school master to the higher echelons of the education field. I should have known.

The incident I intend making mention of occurred in 1929, I believe, at Green School. A furnace in the basement was the only modern convenience we had. I can't remember if we had electricity. I know we didn't have it at our home. There was no phone and no running water. So, naturally, we had an outside well and pump. And outside toilets. One building. Boys on one side and girls on the other. The outhouse figures in my story.

A barber friend of mine, name of Doug, posed a rhetorical question to me that I didn't choose to attempt to dignify with an answer. He wanted to know why men could build houses, practically sound-proof and air tight, so that no air could get in or out. Yet, he'd never seen an outhouse, except a red brick one, and they're rare, that didn't have cracks in the siding—some an inch wide. But Doug's partner, Roger, had the answer. "It's simple," he said. "They needed ventilation."

Moving right along . . . .

On this particular afternoon, Mr. Hostetler had an announcement to make. After he had everybody's attention he told the girls to leave the school room. Just the girls. They were to play in the school yard until he called them back in. He then told the boys there had been some trouble and in order to get it out in the open he wanted to talk to each boy in private.

The only room that afforded any privacy was the area inside the front door which also served as a cloakroom. This room made it so you didn't come directly from the outside into the classroom. When somebody opened the outside door in winter, there was a blast of cold air hitting you in the back of the neck. High winds, two foot of snow, 20 degrees below zero or a combination of all three was no excuse for missing school. We thought it was just normal winter weather. At that time of my life, I didn't really believe there was such a place as Florida.

Mr. Hostetler placed two chairs, facing each other, in the cloak room. That's where he conducted the interrogations. Big boys first. Starting from the front of the room in the eighth grade the first boy was called out to the cloakroom. When he came back into the classroom the next in the row went out and so on. Nobody seemed to know what was happening. Since I was only in the second grade, it took quite a while before it was my turn. It seemed like an eternity. The suspense hung like a pall over the room.

Finally, the boy in front of me finished his turn. I had a real uneasy feeling when I stepped into the cloakroom and closed the door. "Sit down, Ted." I did. Quickly. Partly because my knees felt rubbery. "Ted, I want you to be honest with me when I ask you some questions that need an answer."

"Oh! I will, I will." And I intended to.

He came right to the point. "Mr. Kohlmeyer (he was our County School Superintendent) is very conservative in his distribution of school supplies. So, we need to be careful to not waste any of them. Don't we?"

"Oh, yes!" I replied. Right at the minute the only thing I could think of that Mr. Kohlmeyer furnished for the school was chalk and wood or kerosene.

163

"Well," he continued, "some of the boys have been throwing toilet paper down the hole without using it. Are you one of those boys?"

"No! Not me! No!" And I hadn't. At our house, store-bought toilet paper was a luxury and you didn't waste it. We depended on Sears Roebuck and "Monkey" Ward, as Dad called them, to furnish us with an ample supply of catalogues to use for that purpose.

"Ted, you know that you'll be punished if you lie to me, don't you?"

"Yes, I do. But, I'm not lying," I protested.

Mr. Hostetler leaned closer and continued. "Some of the older boys said you were one who had wasted toilet paper. Now, I want the truth and I want it now or you'll be punished."

To this day I can remember the confused thoughts that rushed through my mind. All I could think of was that I didn't want a "belting." It seemed to my young and, at this point, desperate mind that I'd better tell him what he seemed to be convinced was the truth. Tell him what he wanted to hear and I'd be out of this predicament. I thought. But, not so. I don't know how long the questioning and the protestations of innocence lasted, but I finally relented and said I'd done it. Then, I was told to go back to my seat and send the next boy out.

When all the boys had been to the cloakroom Mr. Hostetler called the girls back into the school room. After everybody was seated and quiet, Mr. Hostetler made the following announcement (to the best of my recollection) "The Bible tells us that it's a sin to tell a lie. Liars must be punished."

Walking over to the storage cupboard he opened the door, stepped up onto the stool to reach the very top shelf, and brought down his factory made leather paddle. This instrument was enough to strike terror into the heart of any boy. It was two inches wide, at least a quarter inch think and 18 inches long, not counting the handle grip.

"Vernon Neff! Step forward." Twelve strokes. Delivered.

"Clarence Seany! Step forward." Twelve strokes. Delivered.

"Ted Woodworth! Step forward." Twelve strokes. Delivered.

"Now, I hope it is understood. I will not permit lying to go unpunished at Green School." This was a dark day for the three of us. "Thrashed" before the entire school!

But every dark cloud has a silver lining. As it happened, all three of us were innocent. Somehow, I've always believed that Amos knew we weren't guilty. So, he punished us for not having enough intestinal fortitude to stick to our original story. The big boys, who were probably the guilty ones, were punished by feelings of guilt for what they had done to us. None of us, after a few days, ever bore a grudge or any ill will toward Amos Hostetler. Oh, yes! What was the silver lining? The three of us learned a valuable lesson that we've carried the rest of our lives: "If you're innocent, don't plead guilty."

49

"Wash Your Mouth Out with Soap, Ted!"

*T*his story could just as well be titled, "How times have changed." But then, so could most of my stories. I'd like to think all my stories have a moral. I intend it that way.

In a semi-monthly magazine published in 54 languages with an average printing of 11,350,000, I read in the following article:

Conditions in the Schools

"The moral decay of society has seriously damaged the ability of schools to teach. It has made it almost impossible for them to provide moral guidance.

Illustrating the changing school environment is the list of the 7 top disciplinary problems in U.S. public schools in 1940 as compared with the top 17 in 1982.

"The 1940 top problems in school were:
(1) talking,
(2) chewing gum,
(3) making noise,
(4) running in the halls,
(5) getting out of turn in line,
(6) wearing improper clothing, and
(7) not putting paper in wastebaskets.

"On the other hand, the 1982 top problems in school were
(1) rape,
(2) robbery,
(3) assault,
(4) burglary,
(5) arson,
(6) bombings,
(7) murder,
(8) suicide,
(9) absenteeism,
(10) vandalism,

(11) extortion,
(12) drug abuse,
(13) alcohol abuse,
(14) gang warfare,
(15) pregnancy,
(16) abortion, and
(17) venereal disease."

There's got to be a message in this. Would it be a lack of discipline? Years ago, teachers had almost a free reign to administer discipline when they thought it necessary. Parents were likewise swift to mete out punishment for rules infractions. Perhaps it boils down to a lack of respect for one's elders. As this respect has been allowed to fall by the wayside—being replaced by disrespect—discipline has disappeared with it.

Now, I don't mean for a minute to imply this is the fault of the teachers. In 1940 you never heard of a teacher being prosecuted for spanking one of his or her students. But now? It happens all the time. If children truly respected their teachers they would realize the old saying, "Spare the rod and spoil the child" applied to teachers as well as parents. It's all in a matter of attitude.

When we are children, our parents and our teachers are the ones in authority. It stands to reason that if we are not taught respect for parents and teachers, we are going to have a real problem when we leave school and join the labor force. Our boss and police, for example, are the ones in authority. Are we going to respect them? Not if we failed to respect our parents and our teachers.

As an example of how times have changed, years ago children used the respectful titles Aunt and Uncle when appropriate. Now you hear some youngsters being permitted to call their aunts and uncles and even their parents by their given name. Maybe the old saying "Familiarity breeds contempt" would apply here.

It has been a gradual change and, admittedly, many children today are respectful to their elders. It's unfair to generalize, because there are lots of young people who still make their parents proud. And they make their teachers proud, also.

It'll never happen, but I wonder if we wouldn't be better off if we were to return to "Readin' and 'Ritin' and 'Rithmetic, Taught to the Tune of the Hickory Stick." I don't remember anybody dying from a thrashing in school. I do know of a rule that was reasonably universal at the time. It was "if you get a spanking by the teacher, you get another when you get home." Usually harder.

After Amos Hostetler spanked me for wasting toilet paper, I expected to be whipped again when I got home. As it happened, I didn't get another. I was able to convince my parents that I hadn't been guilty. However, they never questioned the teacher's right to whip me.

A couple of days after the "whaling" Mr. Hostetler gave us, Vernon Neff, Clarence Seany and I were sitting under a tree plotting our revenge. We had just about decided on putting some thumb tacks on his chair when "lightning struck." I had just said, "He'll be darn sorry for what he did to us," when he suddenly appeared. Now, I've long known that teachers and parents alike have eyes in the backs of their heads, but he had been nowhere near us. Couldn't have seen what we were talking about. Keen ears. That's what it was.

Into the school house he carried me. In the cloakroom he said, "There's a basin of water and there's a cake of soap. Wash your mouth out with soap, Ted."

"But, I didn't do anything," I protested.

"Yes, you did."

"What did I do?"

"You swore. You said 'darn' and I will not allow swearing in my school."

And I washed my mouth out with soap. Nowadays, students use *much* worse language in front of and even to their teachers, and nothing happens.

Amos tried to teach us Bible principles, such as in this case I think he was applying, "The person faithful in what is least is faithful also in much, and the person unrighteous in what is least is unrighteous also in much." Amos Hostetler's way was best.

50

Our Horse, Barney

I saw him! I saw Barney! Beautiful, shiny, brown Barney. Just as sleek and graceful as I remembered him to be 60 years ago. He was pulling one of those sporty one-seater Amish buggies. Trotting along with his tail extended stiff and straight behind him, he looked proud and sure of himself. Hadn't changed one bit since he made so many of us happy back on the farm.

But—was it Barney? After 60 years? No. Sadly, no.

During a month spent in Indiana this summer, I must have seen a dozen horses that made me think of Barney. But then, the Amish have many outstanding horses of which they are justifiably proud.

Actually, there could never be another like Barney. My brothers and the neighbor kids, especially Byron Foltz, got many hours of pleasure out of riding Barney. Sometimes they'd put on a saddle Grandpa Woodworth had given my brother Lloyd. Mostly they rode bareback. Barney seemed to prefer it that way.

Lloyd used to talk about taking Barney to the track at Shipshewana and racing him, but he never did. The only time he was given an opportunity to run at "full tilt" was on the road that ran in front of the Foltz farm and ours. It was just beautiful to see him at full gallop.

Barney was always very gentle with children. We took advantage of that.

I remember our riding him back to the field where the big mulberry tree grew. Pretending to be circus performers, we'd stand on his back to pick mulberries. He was likewise very co-operative when we picked apples because he was paid for his services in apples.

Nothing can make much more noise than a horse eating a crisp apple. Well, I guess maybe a horse eating corn would be noisier, but not much.

Barney had a partner whose name was Prince. They made an odd looking team. They weren't even the same color. Barney was brown while Prince was white. I'll never know why Dad named them the way he did. Barney was such a sleek aristocratic horse while Prince was a tall, raw-boned, gangly horse. Seems like their names should have been reversed.

It's true they worked well together in harness. Barney was always the leader and seemed, at times, to be telling Prince, "Come on now. You're not pulling hard enough." But, otherwise, they got along right well.

Prince would let us ride him, but the bony ridge across his back was most uncomfortable, so he was seldom ridden.

Barney had good balance, too. In the fall, during walnut gathering time, his balance and co-operation came in mighty handy. Not too long after the first hard freeze, my brothers and I would gather together big piles of walnuts. My brothers would climb the trees to shake them down. We tried to put just enough in each pile to fill a gunny sack. After they were sacked and tied, it was time for Barney to help. The bags were carefully placed on Barney's back. About four burlap bags were all that would fit. The boys would kind of wiggle the bags around until they fit all the contours of Barney's back. He would then walk with great care as he carried the bags to the house where they could be "husked" or "hulled" and then dried. We spent a good deal of time cracking black walnuts during the long months of winter.

Another very pleasant memory has stayed with me all these years. All four of us were riding Barney, bareback, in the woods. Since I was the smallest, I was in front. Now, I can't remember how long we had imposed upon Barney, but it was probably quite a long while. Finally, he had had enough of four boisterous boys. Spying a low hanging limb that would have hit me right in the face, Barney headed for it and walked under it. I didn't duck. Instead, I grabbed the limb and hung on for dear life, dragging my three brothers off behind me, because Barney hadn't stopped. Nor did he stop until he was all the way to the barn. He'd had enough of us and didn't care who knew it. My brothers were so carried away with laughing and rolling in the grass they weren't aware of me still hanging in the tree.

Those were carefree days.

Early in the spring of 1931 I experienced one of the most traumatic happenings of my life. Maybe just plain shock would be a better word. Which ever, it was like a bad dream.

While playing in the school yard, during afternoon recess, I became aware of a team of horses moving slowly but steadily toward the school. Because of the road they were on, it was obvious the rig was coming from either the Foltz farm or ours.

Finally, I could see it was Barney and Prince, pulling a wagon, loaded high with farming tools. The driver wore a dark coat and a slouched black hat. He looked sinister to me and as he passed in front of the school house a cold chill seemed to grip me. Since I had never seen this mysterious-looking man before, something told me I would never see him or our horses and wagon or our possessions again.

Times were hard for most folks during those early depression years, but as is true with many poor children, I didn't know just how bad they were until I silently said "good-by" to my friend Barney. I was sure they had been sold.

But, they hadn't. My father had borrowed $25 from a finance company. Because he couldn't make the agreed payments, they had foreclosed. They took our team and wagon as well as all of our possessions they could load on the wagon.

No need to explain the moral of this story. "Neither a borrower nor a lender be."